VISUAL QUICKSTART GUIDE

Word 6

FOR MACINTOSH

David Browne

Peachpit Press

Word 6 for Macintosh: Visual QuickStart Guide
David Browne

Peachpit Press
2414 Sixth Street
Berkeley, CA 94710
510/548-4393
510/548-5991 (fax)

Find us on the World Wide Web at: http://www.peachpit.com

Peachpit Press is a division of Addison Wesley Longman
Publishing Company

Copyright © 1994 by David Browne

Notice of Rights

Notice of Liability

ISBN 1–56609–125–X

9 8 7 6 5 4 3

Printed and bound in the United States of America

Dedication

To Sally, Michael and Kathleen; for the time you gave me to think about and write this book.

Acknowledgements

Somewhere I once read that it's bad form to thank your editor. I've never held by that, and I can't think of anyone more deserving of an author's appreciation than my editor at Peachpit, Roslyn Bullas. You are unflappable; serene in the face of late pages, late betas and (probably) late nights. It's been an absolute pleasure, Roslyn.

Thanks also to Ted Nace at Peachpit. I've thoroughly enjoyed writing about such a fine product, for such a fine organization as yours.

Here's to all the folks at Redmond, their faces lit by the glow of computer monitors, Coke cans stacked to the ceiling, whose imagination and vision created this latest version of Word—a fitting tribute to its tenth anniversary.

Finally, I am in deep debt to my darling wife Sally, who took over the 2 a.m. feeding of baby Kathleen so I could be coherent enough to write. I can only imagine how long I'll be repaying this obligation.

Table of Contents

Chapter 3: **Format the Page**

Table of Contents

Chapter 8: **Word Time Savers**

Chapter 9: **Styles**

Table of Contents

Get Started

WELCOME to Word 6.0 for Macintosh, a powerful word processor. Word is easy to use and smart enough to save you time and energy in creating useful, attractive, and professional documents. Word has so many ways to save you time it just about sits up and begs to help, with features like:

- **AutoCorrect**—catches your typos as you make them and corrects them automatically.

- **AutoFormat**—handles the chores of formatting your document automatically.

- **AutoText**—adds whatever text or graphics you want, where you want it, automatically.

- **Custom ToolBars**—let you create buttons that add text or graphics, or do specific jobs.

- **Format Painter**—effortlessly copies the formats of text or paragraphs and lets you "paint" unformatted text with the same formatting.

- **Forms ToolBar**—creates complex forms with the click of the mouse.

- **Wizards**—handle the tasks of layout and design for you.

Plus, Word has many other automatic features, like figure captions, table formats, borders, numbered headings, bulletted lists, envelopes and labels, and much more. Now, if it could just write the words for you...

About this Book

This Visual QuickStart Guide cuts right to the chase: pictures and descriptions that teach you how to use Word as quickly as possible. Think of it as a no-frills visual presentation on the subject: You get the steps you need along with examples of actual screens, menus and dialog boxes.

There is a fine line between struggling with an application like Word and the quiet confidence that comes with a thorough exposure to the software. While you may be new to computers and word processing software, stick with me through the first few chapters—you'll find using Word can be as comfortable as your favorite easy chair.

Introduction

Word's Document Window

Open a new document in Word and you'll see the new document window with Word's vast array of tools (**Figure 1**).

Word's Document Window

Document title bar **1**
Menu bar **2**
Close box **3**

Standard toolbar **4**
Formatting toolbar **5**
Horizontal Ruler **6**

Zoom box **7**

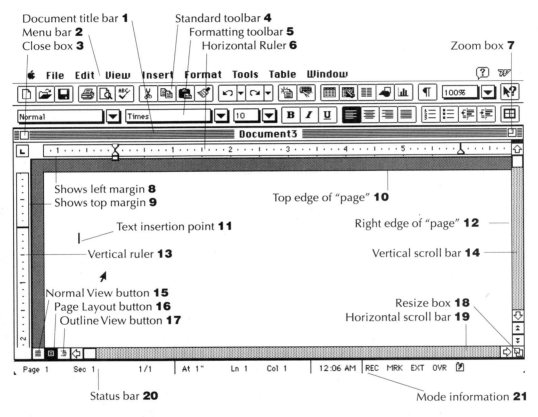

Shows left margin **8**
Shows top margin **9**

Top edge of "page" **10**

Text insertion point **11**

Right edge of "page" **12**

Vertical ruler **13**

Vertical scroll bar **14**

Normal View button **15**
Page Layout button **16**
Outline View button **17**

Resize box **18**
Horizontal scroll bar **19**

Status bar **20**

Mode information **21**

Figure 1 *The different parts to Word's document window.*

Document Window Explained

1 **Document title bar**—The name you assign to the document appears in the title bar. Click and drag the title bar to move the document window on your computer screen.

2 **Menu bar**—The menu bar holds the command menus. The menus drop down when clicked to show the commands that control Word.

3 **Close box**—Closes the application (or window or dialog box) when clicked.

4 **Standard toolbar**—Holds buttons that activate commands on the menu bar. Word comes with many preconfigured toolbars, or you can create your own custom toolbars for specific uses.

5 **Formatting toolbar**—Gives you quick control over text formatting.

6 **Horizontal ruler**—Represents the width of the document "page," the ruler shows tab and indent settings.

7 **Zoom box**—Click to enlarge or reduce the size of the document window.

8 **Shows left margin**—In Word's document layout view, the horizontal ruler shows the left margin assigned to the page. You can also change the margin value using the ruler.

9 **Shows top margin**—Similarly, the vertical ruler indicates the top page margin.

10 **Top edge of "page"**—In layout view, the top edge is shown when the insertion point is near the top margin.

11 **Text insertion point**—Actually a vertical bar not a point, the insertion point shows where text or objects will be typed or inserted.

12 **Right edge of "page"**—The layout view also shows the right edge of the page.

13 **Vertical ruler**—In the layout view, the vertical ruler helps you align text and objects on the page.

14 **Vertical scroll bar**—Word splices its pages together into a long roll. The vertical scroll bar lets you move forward (down) or backward (up) through your document's pages.

15 **Normal View button**—The default view in Word, use the Normal view to type and edit text.

16 **Page Layout button**—Shown in Figure 1, the Layout view is a WYSIWYG rendering of part of the page (about 1/3 at 100 percent zoom).

17 **Outline View button**—A special view, with a specialized toolbar, for creating and revising outlines.

18 **Size box**—Click and drag the box to resize the document window to any new proportion. Unlike the Zoom box which allows only two sizes, the Size box lets you tailor just the size you want.

19 **Horizontal scroll bar**—Slide the page sideways, left or right, with this scroll bar.

20 **Status bar**—An area at the bottom of your screen that gives you help and information based on what you're doing at the moment.

21 **Mode information**—*Record* a macro, *mark* revisions to a document, *extend* a selection through a large amount of text, or type in *Overtype* instead of *Insert* mode.

Document Window Explained

Using Word's Menus

The command menus in Word's menu bar hold the commands that control the application and most of Word's functionality. Each menu drops down, showing the commands it contains when clicked with the mouse arrow.

To open a menu, position the mouse pointer over the menu you want to open, click and hold the mouse button. The menu will drop down. To choose a command, continue pressing the mouse button and slide the pointer down the menu to the command you want. Release the mouse button.

Some commands may have symbols **(Figure 2)** that indicate specific information:

- **Keyboard Shortcuts**—an equivalent keyboard combination to invoke the command. Sometimes it's faster to use a keyboard shortcut than to click a command with the mouse.

- **Ellipsis**—or three periods after the command mean a dialog box will open if you click the command.

- **Right arrow**—indicates a submenu will open if you choose the command.

- **Dimmed commands**—the command is grayed out, or dimmed if it's not available (you may have to select text, for example, before the command becomes active).

- **Check marks**—a check mark beside a command means that the command is toggled on; to toggle it off, simply choose the check-marked command to remove the check mark.

How keyboard shortcuts are shown in this book

Shortcuts are combination keystrokes, involving the Command or Shift keys and another key on the keyboard. To use a shortcut, hold down the first key (Command or Shift) and momentarily press the second key. Shortcuts shown on menus will look like:

⌘C (meaning hold down the Command key and press C)

⌘⇧3 (meaning hold down the Command and Shift keys and press 3).

In this book, shortcuts are shown as **Cmd+C**, or **Cmd+Shift+3**.

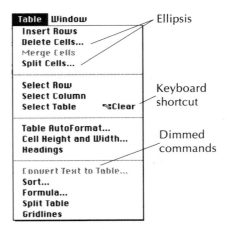

Figure 2 *Menu command symbols.*

Menus

File Menu

Creating, managing and saving files are handled by commands on the File menu **(Figure 3)**. The File menu lists the most recent documents you have worked in and displays their file names at the bottom of the menu.

Notice the Save All command, which saves all open documents at once; the Find File command, that finds those pesky documents that are hiding somewhere in the magnetic recesses of your hard disk; and the Templates command that reveals a wealth of templates, ready for use.

Edit Menu

Here are the basic editing commands **(Figure 4)**: cut, copy, paste and clear; and the all-important Undo command that has saved my bacon more than once. Paste Special isn't a sale on paste, but rather a way to establish a link between Word and the source of the pasted object.

You will find the AutoText command here, although I think it should be on the Tools menu (read Appendix A to find out how to move the command to a different menu).

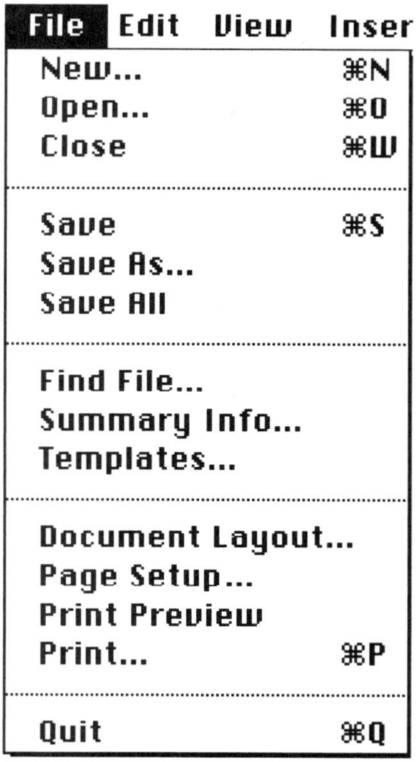

File	Edit	View	Inser
New...			⌘N
Open...			⌘O
Close			⌘W
Save			⌘S
Save As...			
Save All			
Find File...			
Summary Info...			
Templates...			
Document Layout...			
Page Setup...			
Print Preview			
Print...			⌘P
Quit			⌘Q

Figure 3 *File Menu.*

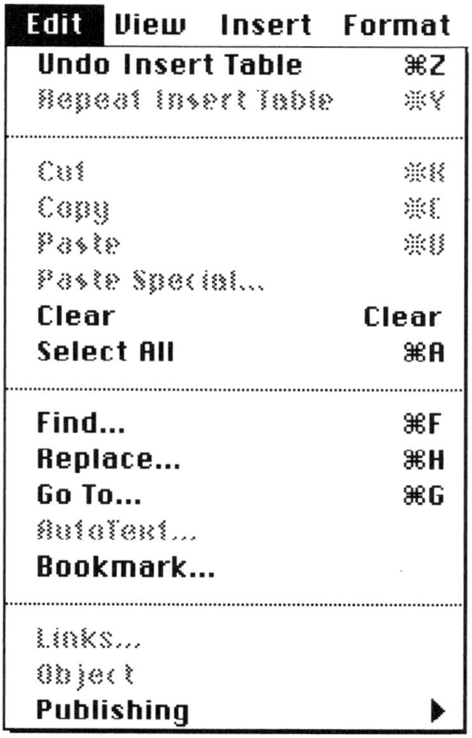

Edit	View	Insert	Format
Undo Insert Table			⌘Z
Repeat Insert Table			⌘Y
Cut			⌘X
Copy			⌘C
Paste			⌘V
Paste Special...			
Clear			Clear
Select All			⌘A
Find...			⌘F
Replace...			⌘H
Go To...			⌘G
AutoText...			
Bookmark...			
Links...			
Object			
Publishing			▶

Figure 4 *Edit Menu.*

View Menu

This menu **(Figure 5)** lets you "see" all sorts of things, such as different toolbars, the Ruler, headers and footers, footnotes, and annotations. The Zoom command gives you a variety of magnifications and reductions of the pages. Most importantly, this menu provides different views of the page, including Normal (for word processing) Outline (for quick, efficient outlines) and Page Layout (for desktop layout and publishing).

Insert Menu

This menu **(Figure 6)** displays some of the things you can insert into your documents, from hidden codes like page breaks, to special symbols like the trademark and copyright symbols, to whole spreadsheets, database query results or graphic images.

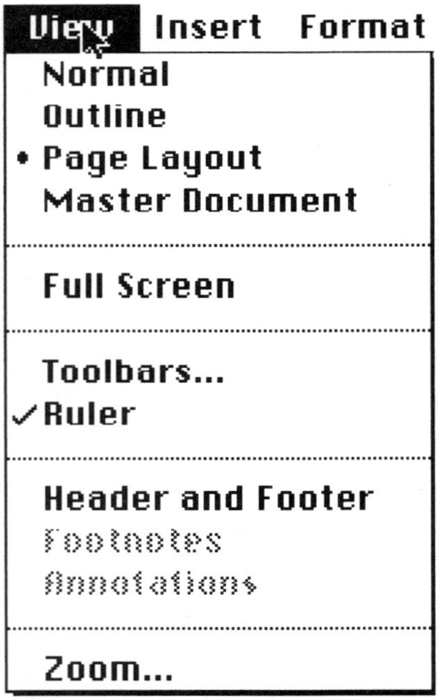

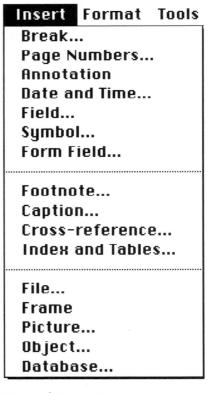

Figure 5 *View Menu.*

Figure 6 *Insert Menu.*

Format Menu

For help in refining and improving the look of your document, use the Format menu **(Figure 7)**. The Font, Paragraph and Tabs commands handle the normal tasks of arranging words on the page. Borders, drop caps, bullets, and numbering for headings and paragraphs are handled through virtually automatic dialog boxes. AutoFormat politely formats your documents for you, while the Style Gallery makes available the professional styles that come with Word.

Tools Menu

Check the spelling, grade your grammar, find antonyms and synonyms, choose a different language to write in, even correct common typing and punctuation mistakes automatically—all these and more are handled by the Tools menu **(Figure 8)**. You can print envelopes and mailing labels with the click of the mouse, record and play back macros and customize the look and feel of Word to your exact liking.

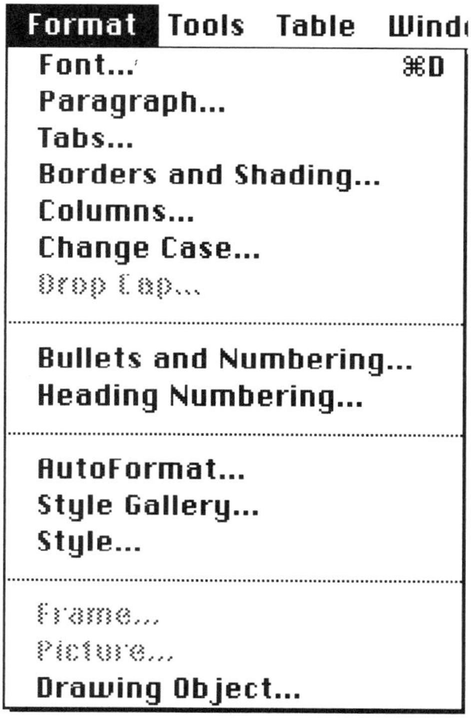

Format Tools Table Wind(	
Font...	⌘D
Paragraph...	
Tabs...	
Borders and Shading...	
Columns...	
Change Case...	
Drop Cap...	
Bullets and Numbering...	
Heading Numbering...	
AutoFormat...	
Style Gallery...	
Style...	
Frame...	
Picture...	
Drawing Object...	

Figure 7 *Format Menu.*

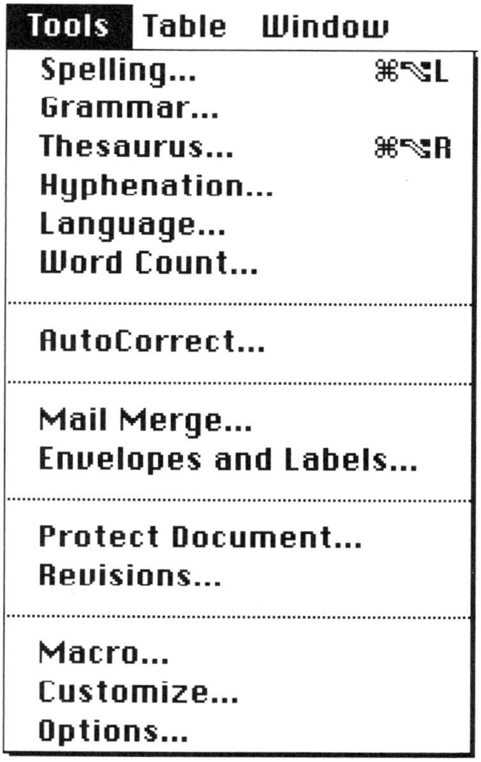

Tools Table Window	
Spelling...	⌘⌥L
Grammar...	
Thesaurus...	⌘⌥R
Hyphenation...	
Language...	
Word Count...	
AutoCorrect...	
Mail Merge...	
Envelopes and Labels...	
Protect Document...	
Revisions...	
Macro...	
Customize...	
Options...	

Figure 8 *Tools Menu.*

Menus

Table Menu

You'll find everything you need to create effective tables using the Table menu **(Figure 9)**. Especially useful are commands like Table AutoFormat (creates attractive tables with the click of the mouse), Headings (controls and defines table column headings) and Convert Text to Table (which automatically converts tabbed text to a table).

Toolbars

Toolbars are shortcuts to the commands on menus. One click of a button on the toolbar is the equivalent to clicking to open the menu and clicking the command you want on the menu. Let's say you want to work on an existing document: instead of clicking the File menu and choosing the Open command to see the Open dialog box, simply click the Open button on the toolbar.

Word comes already set up with two toolbars located under the menu bar. The Standard toolbar **(Figure 10)** offers buttons for many of the commands used in creating documents. The Formatting toolbar **(Figure 11)** gives you quick access to changing the look and style of text on the page. Besides the default toolbars, Word has a number of specialized toolbars designed for working in specific areas, such as with imported databases, drawings and charts, forms or other Microsoft applications.

Opening More Toolbars

1 Choose the View menu **(Figure 12)** by moving the mouse pointer over the menu and clicking.

2 Drag the pointer down the menu to select Toolbars. You will see the Toolbars dialog box **(Figure 13)**.

3 Click the empty option boxes for those toolbars you want to display. To close a toolbar, click the checked box to remove the **X**.

4 Click the OK button to return to your document.

Word's available toolbars are shown in **Figures 14 - 19** beginning on page 10.

Table   Window

> Insert Rows
> Delete Cells...
> Merge Cells
> Split Cells...
>
> Select Row
> Select Column
> Select Table   ↖Clear
>
> Table AutoFormat...
> Cell Height and Width...
> Headings
>
> Convert Text to Table...
> Sort...
> Formula...
> Split Table
> Gridlines

Figure 9 *Table Menu.*

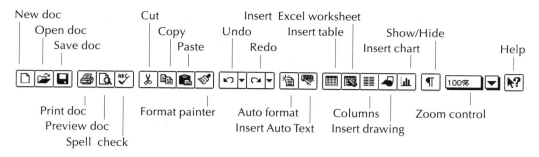

Figure 10 *Word's default Standard toolbar.*

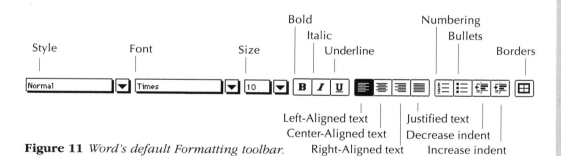

Figure 11 *Word's default Formatting toolbar.*

Toolbars

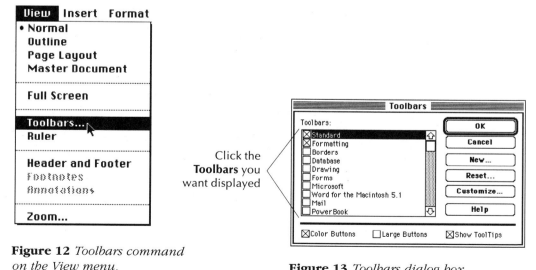

Figure 12 *Toolbars command on the View menu.*

Figure 13 *Toolbars dialog box.*

Sets line thickness Top border Bottom border Left side border No border Sets line shading

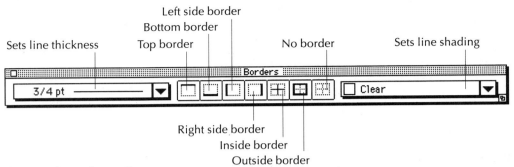

Right side border
Inside border
Outside border

Figure 14 *Border toolbar.*

Data form Manage fields Sort ascending Sort descending Find record Mail merge main document

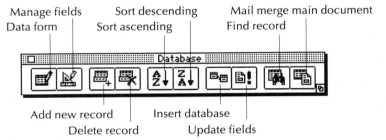

Add new record
Delete record
Insert database
Update fields

Figure 15 *Database toolbar.*

Line Rectangle Ellipse Arc Freeform Text box Callout Format callout Fill color Line color Line style Select objects

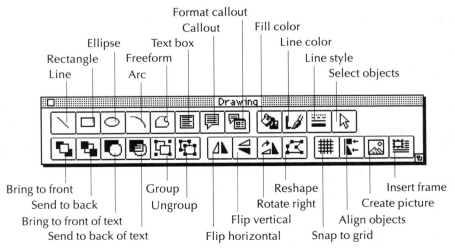

Bring to front
Send to back
Bring to front of text
Send to back of text
Group Ungroup
Flip horizontal
Flip vertical Reshape Rotate right
Snap to grid Align objects
Create picture Insert frame

Figure 16 *Drawing toolbar.*

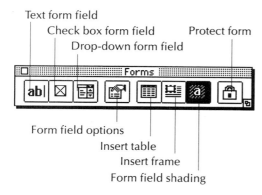

Text form field
Check box form field
Drop-down form field
Protect form

Form field options
Insert table
Insert frame
Form field shading

Figure 17 *Forms toolbar.*

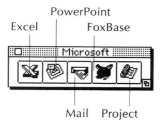

Excel
PowerPoint
FoxBase

Mail   Project

Figure 18 *Microsoft applications toolbar.*

Figure 19 *ToolTip appears identifying the button.*

About ToolTips

As you can see, there are a lot of buttons on the toolbars to remember. The button icons will often jog your memory, but Word helps you even more with clever button name hints, called *ToolTips*. If you keep the mouse pointer over a button for more than two seconds, you'll see a small name tag appear with the name of the button. Once the ToolTip appears for that button, you'll see it instantly for any other button on the toolbar. ToolTips are a great way to get familiar with the buttons on the different toolbars.

Using ToolTips

1 Move the mouse arrow up to the Standard or Formatting toolbar and position it over any button or list box. Wait for a second or two.

2 A small, identifying label will appear directly below the button **(Figure 19)**.

3 Now, move the mouse arrow to any other button on the toolbar and you'll see its ToolTip immediately appear.

Once the mouse pointer is moved off and back on the toolbar, ToolTips will again be initially delayed before appearing. (See Appendix A for more information about modifying toolbar buttons.)

Toolbars; ToolTips

Shortcut Menus

Word knows that sometimes you'd like instant access to just a few specialized commands based on what you're doing. Shortcut menus are just that: shortcuts around the lengthy menus on the menu bar that are task-oriented. You can see a specific shortcut menu anytime by holding down the Control key and clicking the mouse button (called a Ctrl+click). Here are a few examples:

- **List shortcut menu**—is handy for sorting and organizing lists **(Figure 20)**. Click the insertion point anywhere in the list and Ctrl+click to see the menu.

- **Paragraph shortcut menu**—helps you quickly format paragraphs **(Figure 21)**. Click anywhere in the paragraph you want to modify, and Ctrl+click to open the menu.

- **Frame shortcut menu**—handles the look and arrangement of frames **(Figure 22)**. Click the frame to select it and Ctrl+click to see the menu.

- **Table shortcut menu**—lets you quickly modify the size and style of tables **(Figure 23)**. This shortcut menu gives you access to the Table AutoFormat command, a fast, powerful time-saver. Click anywhere in the table and Ctrl+click to open the menu.

- **Toolbar shortcut menu**—gives you instant access to the list of Word's toolbars **(Figure 24)**. Move the mouse pointer over any toolbar that's open, including the two built-in toolbars at the top of the document window, and Ctrl+click to open the menu.

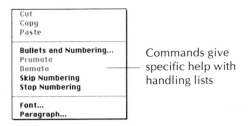

Commands give specific help with handling lists

Figure 20 *List shortcut menu.*

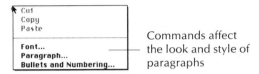

Commands affect the look and style of paragraphs

Figure 21 *Paragraph shortcut menu.*

Frame-oriented commands

Figure 22 *Frame shortcut menu.*

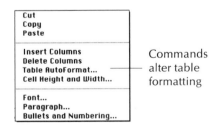

Commands alter table formatting

Figure 23 *Table shortcut menu.*

Figure 24 *Toolbar shortcut menu.*

Using the Mouse

If this is your first experience with the Macintosh, you may find using the mouse to be a bit awkward. Don't despair, by the end of this chapter you'll feel like an old pro with the mouse. So far you've done a bit of pointing and clicking (or Ctrl+clicking), but the mouse is capable of controlling Word in many different ways.

- **Clicking**—a momentary press and release of the mouse button. Clicking opens menus and selects commands, activates buttons and options, and positions the text insertion point where you want to type.

- **Highlighting**—press and hold down the mouse button and move the insertion point across the text you want to highlight. The highlighted text will be reversed out of a black bar. Once highlighted, you can type new text to replace it, or press the Delete key.

- **Double-clicking**—two clicks in quick succession. Double-clicking a word highlights it.

- **Drag and drop**—*drag* means to click and highlight text and move the mouse to the position you want. When you release the button the text will be *dropped* into position (faster than using the Cut and Paste commands).

- **Selecting**—choose the item you want in a list box, or on a menu, by clicking the item or command. Select a box or frame with a click of the mouse.

- **Adjusting sizes**—frames and boxes show sizing handles when selected. To adjust the size, click a sizing handle, press and hold the mouse button, and drag to change the dimension.

Press and release

Position insertion point

Click and drag

Text is highlighted

Quickly press and release twice

Loaded box means dragging the pointer will move what was highlighted

Position the arrow and click once to select the choice

Locate the arrow over a sizing handle and it shows the direction of adjustment

Sizing handles

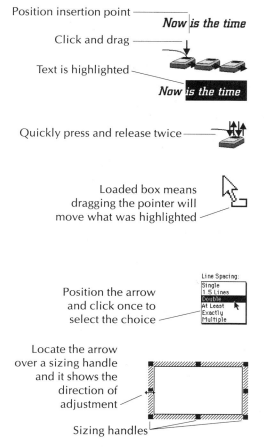

Using Dialog Boxes

Dialog boxes are floating windows that pop up when you choose a command on a menu or press a keyboard shortcut. They are your means of communicating with Word (and the Macintosh) and packed with quick tools to help you select and define your needs **(Figure 25)**:

■ **Pop-up menus**—are indicated by a shadow box. Click the box to open the menu **(Figure 26)**. You can select any single item on the list by clicking it; some pop-up menus let you select multiple items by holding down the Ctrl key and clicking the items you want.

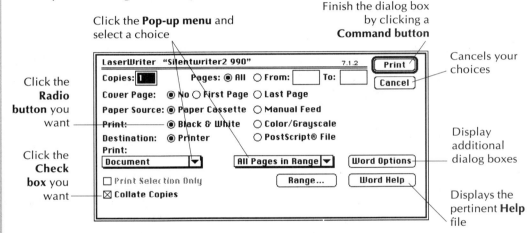

Figure 25 *Word's Print dialog box specifies exactly what to print.*

Print:

Document ▲
✓Document
Summary Info
Annotations
Styles
AutoText Entries
Key Assignments

Figure 26 *Pop-up menus often pop "down."*

Click and type in the **Text box**

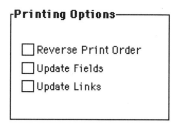

Figure 27 *Using text boxes*

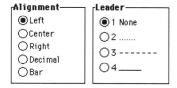

Figure 28 *Click as many check boxes as you want.*

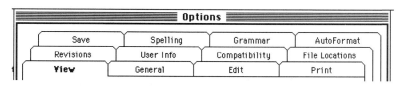

Figure 29 *Tab alignment radio buttons let you make only one choice for alignment and leader style.*

■ **Text boxes**—look like a Pop-up menu without the shadow. Click the arrow inside the text box and you'll see a text insertion point **(Figure 27)**. Type what you want in the box; use Backspace or Delete keys to edit any mistakes.

■ **Check boxes**—are square boxes you click to add an X (the X means the options are activated). Click the check box again to remove the X **(Figure 28)**. In a list of check boxes you may activate as many as you want.

■ **Radio buttons**—are round buttons you click to add a black dot (which means the option is activated). Although you might see a group of radio buttons **(Figure 29)**, they are mutually exclusive, only one can be activated in any group.

■ **Command buttons**—are normally the last buttons you deal with in a dialog box. The command button with a double border (usually the OK button) can be activated by pressing the Return key. Cancel undoes everything you did to the dialog box and takes you back to your document.

■ **Tabs**—separate layered dialog boxes, like tabbed folders organize a file drawer **(Figure 30)**. Click the tab name to move to that dialog box. Each tabbed dialog box has OK and Cancel command buttons—click either when you're through, to go back to your document.

Dialog Boxes

Options			
Save	Spelling	Grammar	AutoFormat
Revisions	User Info	Compatibility	File Locations
View	General	Edit	Print

Figure 30 *Click the tab to move to that dialog box.*

Getting the Best View

Word offers you a number of different views of your work. Use the view most suited for what you want to do. All views are accessed on the View menu **(Figure 31)**.

- **Normal view**—is used for quick typing and formatting **(Figure 32)**. This view gives you an accurate rendering of the page, but hides margins, headers, and footers.

- **Page Layout view**—shows a true WYSIWYG representation of your document pages, including all margins, headers, and footers **(Figure 33)**.

- **Outline view**—displays only major and minor headings in an outline format **(Figure 34)**. This view includes a special Outline toolbar.

- **Master Document view**—is used to assemble subdocuments, like chapters, into a master document **(Figure 35)**. More tools are added to the toolbar to help define, merge, and organize subdocuments.

- **Full Screen view**—fills your screen with your document, without the distractions of the document window **(Figure 36)**.

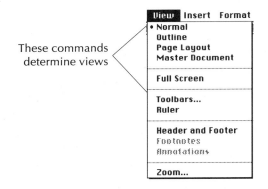

These commands determine views

Figure 31 *View menu.*

Figure 32 *Normal view of document.*

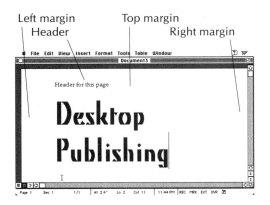

Left margin
Header
Top margin
Right margin
Header for this page

Figure 33 *Page Layout view of document.*

Getting the Best View

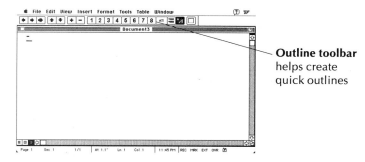

Outline toolbar
helps create
quick outlines

Figure 34 *Outline view of document.*

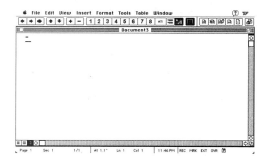

Figure 35 *Master document view of document.*

To go back to the
normal document
window, click the **Full
Screen** button

Figure 36 *Full screen view of document.*

Getting the Best View

Getting Help

Don't worry, there's lots of help in Word:

- **Tips of the Day**—every time you start Word, it presents you with a Tip of the Day window **(Figure 37)**, with helpful tips to make your work easier. Turn off the automatic display of start-up tips by clicking the **Show Tips at Startup** check box to remove the *X*.

- **Wizards**—are clever fellows that guide you through each step in the design and layout of many kinds of documents and tables.

- **User help prompts**—appear at the bottom of the document window whenever you click on a menu, command, or button. You'll see a brief help message that explains what you're about to do.

- **Balloon help**—displays small, comic strip-style dialog balloons of help messages **(Figure 38)** whenever you move the mouse arrow over important parts of the screen. You can activate baleen help by opening the Help menu and clicking **Show Balloons**.

- **Help windows**—Word includes a powerful on-line help system that can offer assistance of virtually any question you may have. Click open the Help menu and choose **Microsoft Word Help** to see the table of contents **(Figure 39)**. Use the contents window to branch to any specific area. Choose **Back** to back up through the help screens you've already seen.

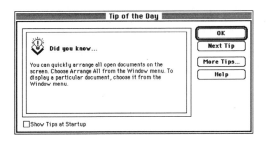

Figure 37 *Tip of the Day Window can be displayed whenever Word starts.*

Figure 38 *Balloon Help appears whenever you position the arrow over important areas of the Macintosh (or Word) screen.*

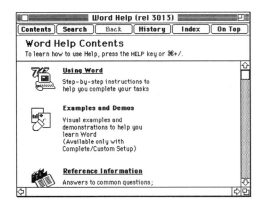

Figure 39 *Word's Help system table of contents leads you to specific help text.*

Add Text

*D*ON'T be concerned if you've never used word processing software before; in many ways it's very similar to typing on a typewriter. For instance, Word's page layout window looks like a sheet of paper, with the margins you specify on the sides, top and bottom. And, as you type on the keyboard, characters are added from left to right on the "page." Here are some rules to remember when using Word:

- Don't press the Return key at the end of each line to move down to the next line. Word handles that automatically. The only time you need to press Return is when you start a new paragraph. Pressing the Return key adds a blank line to the page, which is a quick way to add vertical spacing.

- Don't add two spaces before each sentence. The two space rule is left over from the days of typewriters, where it should stay. Use only one space before sentences in paragraphs, as the double spaces will create some unattractive results.

- Use tabs, not spaces to vertically align words, phrases or numbers. As you'll learn in Chapter 3, while spaces may look aligned, the printed results will be less than satisfactory.

- Don't use spaces to indent the first line of a paragraph. Instead, set a tab or first line indent (Chapter 3).

Think of the pages of your document like Word does: as a series of paragraphs, rather than individual sentences.

How Word Processors Work

Starting Word

1 From your Mac's desktop, open the Word folder **(Figure 1)** by double-clicking it.

2 Now, start Word by double-clicking the Word program icon **(Figure 2)**. You can also start Word by clicking any Word document or template.

3 In a moment, the application will load and you'll see Word's document window. Answer the requisite Tip of the Day and you're ready to begin work.

Tip

■ If you've upgraded from Word's previous version and miss the look of version 5.1, you can change Word's toolbars to resemble the older version. Simply open the View menu and choose Toolbars **(Figure 3)** to display the Toolbars dialog box **(Figure 4)**. Click the **Word for Macintosh 5.1** option box to add an **X**, and click the **Standard** box to remove the **X**. Now, Word 6 will still work the same, but will sport the older ribbon of version 5.1.

Figure 1 *Word folder on the Mac desktop.*

Word's program icon; click to start

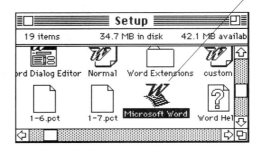

Figure 2 *Word program icon inside the Setup folder.*

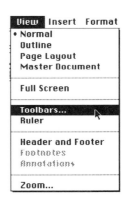

Figure 3 *Toolbars command on the View menu.*

Click **Standard** to remove the X

Click **Word for Mac 5.1** to add an X

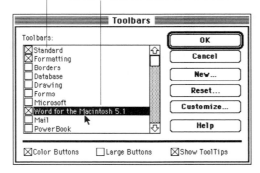

Figure 4 *Toolbars dialog box.*

———Text will always be added
at this symbol

Figure 5 *Text insertion point.*

Current position of the Insertion point

Adding text in Word for Macintosh is easy.

Move the mouse to position the **I-beam**

Adding text in Word for Macintosh is easy.

Click the mouse and the I-beam
changes to the **insertion point**

Adding text in Word for Macintosh is easy.

Now type and the words will be added at the
insertion point position

Adding text in Word for Macintosh Version 6 is easy.

Figure 6 *Move the insertion point by
moving the I-beam.*

Adding Text

1 Type as you normally would on a type-writer. Notice that text is added at the blinking vertical bar **(Figure 5)**, called the **text insertion point**.

2 Once text is added to the document, you can move the insertion point with the mouse by clicking the **I-beam (Figure 6)**. If you prefer, you can also use the arrow keys on the keyboard to move the insertion point. Notice that you can't move the insertion point any further than there are words on the page.

As you type, words are added down the page, and are connected together, bottom-to-top, like a scroll of music in a player piano. Breaks between pages are shown as a single dotted line **(Figure 7)**.

Adding Text

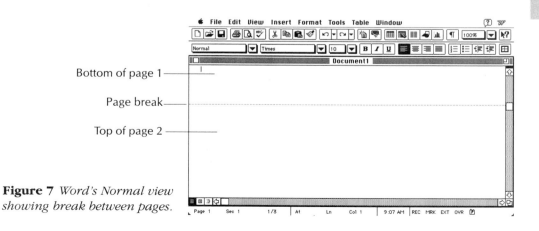

Bottom of page 1 ——

Page break——

Top of page 2 ——

Figure 7 *Word's Normal view
showing break between pages.*

Highlighting Text

Before you can do anything to text, you must first highlight it. For example, to delete more than one character at a time, you must first highlight the text, then press the Backspace or Delete key.

1 Position the I-beam before the first character you want to highlight, press and hold the mouse button and drag the I-beam across all the characters and words you want selected **(Figure 8)**.

2 To highlight words, position the I-beam anywhere in the word and double-click **(Figure 9)**. To highlight a paragraph, triple-click anywhere in the paragraph **(Figure 10)**.

Once highlighted, words can be deleted, copied, moved or formatted **(Figure 11)**.

Tip

■ Use Word's *selection bar* to highlight lines, paragraphs, or whole documents. Move the I-beam to the left margin. When the I-beam changes to a right-facing arrow **(Figure 12)**, you're in the selection bar. Point to a line of type in a paragraph and click once to highlight the line, twice to highlight the whole paragraph, or three times to highlight the complete document.

Figure 8 *Highlight by clicking and dragging the I-beam across characters and spaces.*

Figure 9 *Highlight words by double-clicking.*

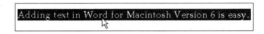

Figure 10 *Highlight paragraphs by triple-clicking.*

Highlighted text is italicized by clicking the Italics button

Figure 11 *Use the **Formatting toolbar** to quickly modify highlighted text.*

Selection bar is the left page margin; click the mouse here to highlight

Figure 12 *Highlight lines of text, paragraphs or whole documents by clicking in the **selection bar** area.*

Overtype mode

| 9:13 AM | REC MRK EXT **OVR** |

Figure 13 *Status bar button controls typing mode.*

Tools Table Window
Spelling...   ⌘⌥L
Grammar...
Thesaurus...   ⌘⌥R
Hyphenation...
Language...
Word Count...

AutoCorrect...

Mail Merge...
Envelopes and Labels...

Protect Document...
Revisions...

Macro...
Customize...
Options...

Figure 14 *Options command on the Tools menu.*

Changing Typing Modes

Normally, Word lets you add words to the page by pushing any text to the right of the insertion point. However, if you're used to typing over existing characters to the right of the insertion point when you add text, change Word's typing mode to *Overtype*.

1 Position the insertion point where you want to add text (by moving the mouse I-beam and clicking where you want it).

2 Move the mouse arrow to the status bar along the bottom of the document window and double-click the **OVR** button **(Figure 13)**. If OVR is dimmed it means Word is in the Insert mode (text to the right is pushed ahead, new text is inserted. When OVR is darkened, the Overtype mode is in effect.

Tip

◼ While this book is written based on using the Insert mode, if you want to permanently use the Overtype mode, choose the Tools menu and click the Options command **(Figure 14)**. In the Options dialog box **(Figure 15)**, click the Edit tab **(Figure 16)** and choose Overtype Mode to add an X.

Typing Modes

Click the **Edit** tab

[Options dialog box - View tab]

Figure 15 *Options dialog box.*

Click **Overtype Mode**

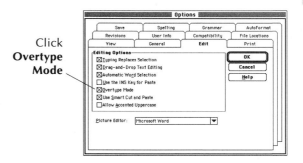

Figure 16 *Edit Tab lets you make Overtype mode permanent.*

Undoing What You Just Did

Click, click, oops! Gosh, I didn't want to do that. To undo your last action, use the Undo command on the Edit menu **(Figure 17)**. This command will undo many commands, as well as text deletions. As a matter of fact, the undo command will tell what it's capable of doing (or undoing) at any given moment. For example, if you type some text, or delete text and open the Edit menu, Undo will say *Undo Typing*. If you assign a style to text and look at the menu, the command will say *Undo Style*, and so forth.

Undoing any Action

Since the Undo command only undoes your last action, Word uses the Undo button on the Standard toolbar **(Figure 18)** to remember virtually all the actions you take.

1 Click the down arrow next to the undo button. You will see a pop-up list of all your actions **(Figure 19)**.

2 Choose the action you want undone.

Tip

◼ Word not only remembers the action, but remembers where the action was taken. So if you moved some text from one paragraph to another several pages back, you needn't return to that location to undo the action. Simply choose the action description from the pop-up menu and the move will be undone.

Figure 17 *Undo command on the Edit menu.*

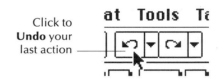

Click to **Undo** your last action

Figure 18 *Undo button on Standard toolbar.*

Click Undo arrow to see all actions that can be undone

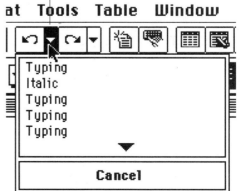

Figure 19 *Choose the Undo action from the pop-up menu.*

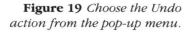

Undoing

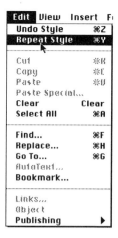

Figure 20 *Repeat command on the Edit menu.*

Click Redo arrow to see list of actions that can be redone

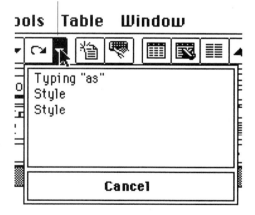

Figure 21 *Repeat pop-up menu on the Standard toolbar.*

Redoing and Repeating

Repeating is the opposite of undoing: you repeat whatever you just did. If your last action included some extensive and complicated formatting to a paragraph, instead of having to remember all the formatting steps for another paragraph, simply click the paragraph and choose the Repeat command on the Edit menu **(Figure 20)**.

Like the Undo command, there is also a Redo button on the toolbar, so if you want to redo what you just undid with the Undo button, click the Redo button. There is a similar Repeat pop-up menu that records a list of all redone actions **(Figure 21)**.

Formatting Text

Word formats characters based on the paragraph they are a part of. To change the format of all words in the paragraph, click anywhere in the paragraph. To change selected words, first highlight the words, then change the formatting.

1 Choose the Format menu and select the Font command **(Figure 22)**. You will see the Font dialog box open **(Figure 23)**.

2 Change the values in the dialog box based on how you want the text to appear.

3 Choose OK to return to your document.

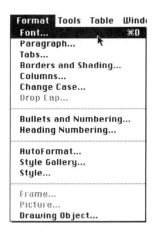

Figure 22 *Font command on the Format menu.*

Font pop-up menu lists the fonts available in your system

Choose a **Font Style** from the list

Choose the **Size** for the font you select

Click to **Save** the settings you make

Click to make the these settings the **Default** settings for new documents

Underline styles add an underscore below selected text

Add **special effects** to your text here

Changes the **Color** of text

Preview window shows the changes you make

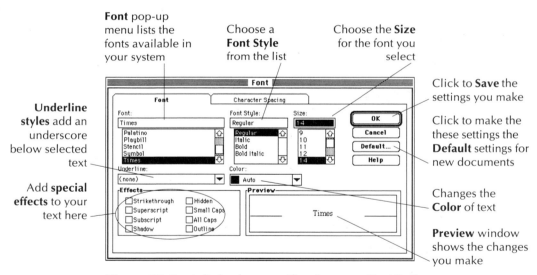

Figure 23 *Font dialog box specifies the exact "look" of the text.*

Formatting Text

Choosing a Font Style

Font styles are different from document styles that are explained in Chapter 9. To change the font style of selected text:

1 Highlight the text you want to change and open the Font dialog box.

2 Choose a font style for your text using the Font Style menu. Usually, the regular style is used for body text; bold and italic are reserved for emphasis and headings or headlines.

Font Style	Description	Example
Regular	The "normal" style of any font	Regular
Italic	A slanted or script version	*Italic*
Bold	Heavier and darker than normal	**Bold**
Bold Italic	Heavier slanted or script version	***Bold Italic***

Figure 24 *Underline style pop-up menu on the Font dialog box.*

Choosing a Line Style

To underline text:

1 Highlight the text you want to underline and open the Font dialog box.

2 Choose an underline style from the Underline style pop-up menu **(Figure 24)**.

Line Style	Description	Example
Single	Single underline, words and spaces	An example
Words only	Single underline of words not spaces	An example
Double	Two underlines of words and spaces	An example
Dotted	Single underline of dots	An example

Changing Text Color

Normally, all text on the page is black. To change the color of text, choose the color you want from the Color pop-up menu in the Font dialog box **(Figure 25)**. Text in a color other than black will print as a shade of gray with a laser printer; you must use a color printer in order to print the colors you choose.

Figure 25 *Color pop-up menu in the Font dialog box.*

Using the Formatting Toolbar

The Formatting toolbar **(Figure 26)** is an easy-to-use alternative to the Font dialog box. With it, you can quickly choose the font you want, the font size and Font style.

Notice that the Italics button on the Formatting toolbar in Figure 26 is darkened. Clicking the buttons once darkens them, activating their features; clicking them again turns the buttons white, turning off their features.

Formatting Keyboard Shortcuts

Another way to quickly format text in your document is with keyboard shortcuts. Simply highlight the text you want to change (or click the paragraph you want formatted) and apply one or more of these key combinations:

Bold	Cmd+B
Italics	Cmd+I
Underline	Cmd+U
Align Left	Cmd+L
Align Right	Cmd+R
Change Font	Cmd+Shift+F
Remove Formatting	Cmd+Shift+Z

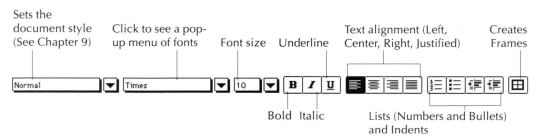

Figure 26 *Do quick text formatting with the Formatting toolbar.*

Sets the document style (See Chapter 9) · Click to see a pop-up menu of fonts · Font size · Underline · Text alignment (Left, Center, Right, Justified) · Creates Frames · Bold Italic · Lists (Numbers and Bullets) and Indents

Formatting Text

Figure 27 *Open command on the File menu.*

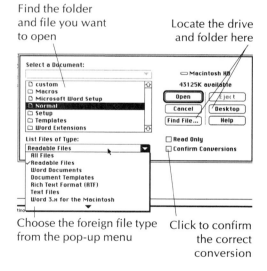

Find the folder and file you want to open

Locate the drive and folder here

Choose the foreign file type from the pop-up menu

Click to confirm the correct conversion

Figure 28 *Choose the file to import in the Open dialog box.*

Importing Text

You may want to use existing text from another document instead of retyping what has already been written. Called *importing* text, Word can "read" a number of types of word processing documents (such as WordPerfect) spreadsheets (like Lotus and Excel) and databases (like dBase and Access).

To Open "Foreign" Files

1 Choose the File menu and select the Open command **(Figure 27)**.

2 In the Open dialog box **(Figure 28)** choose the type of file you want to open from the File type pop-up menu. If you don't see the type of file you want, choose All Files.

3 Select the file from the File Name list and choose OK.

Tips

■ If Word can't recognize the type of file, re-save the foreign file as a simple text file. Saving as a text file will drop any formatting associated with the foreign file, but will ensure Word can read and open the file.

■ If Word can't import the file, open the application that created it and use the Copy command to save it to the Clipboard. Move back to Word and Paste the information into a new document.

■ Word can work just as readily with files from Word 6 for Windows as Word 6 for Macintosh. The first time you save the Windows-version files, Word will ask whether you want to save them in Macintosh or Windows format (remember the maximum 8-character name rule for Windows files).

Importing Text

Inserting a Document

Sometimes you may want to insert an existing document you've already created (whether in Word, or another application) into the document you're writing. Follow these steps:

1 Position the text insertion point where you want to add the document.

2 Choose the Insert menu **(Figure 29)** and select the File command.

3 Use the File dialog box **(Figure 30)** to locate the file you want.

4 Choose OK to insert the file at the insertion point position.

Figure 29 *File command on the Insert menu.*

Find the file you want
to insert

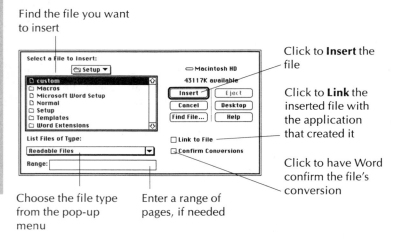

Click to **Insert** the file

Click to **Link** the inserted file with the application that created it

Click to have Word confirm the file's conversion

Choose the file type from the pop-up menu

Enter a range of pages, if needed

Figure 30 *Use the File dialog box to insert a file in your document.*

Inserting Text

Figure 31 *Save command on the File menu.*

Saving Your Work

When first installed, Word is set to automatically save your work for you, every 10 minutes. However, you must save your new documents to assign them names.

1 Choose the File menu **(Figure 31)** and click the Save command (or use the keyboard shortcut **Cmd+S**).

2 Use the Save As dialog box **(Figure 32)** to assign a name to your new document.

3 Choose OK to return to your document.

Once a name is assigned, choosing the Save command, or pressing Cmd+S, will instantly save any changes you make to the document. However, Word will not redisplay the Save dialog box.

Tips

◼ Once you've saved your document, if you find you've made changes you don't like, simply close the document without saving it—the document will revert to the last-saved version.

◼ Word will always remind you to save your open documents whenever you close them or exit the program.

◼ To change the name you have assigned to a document, use the Save As command on the File menu (see Chapter 7 for the steps).

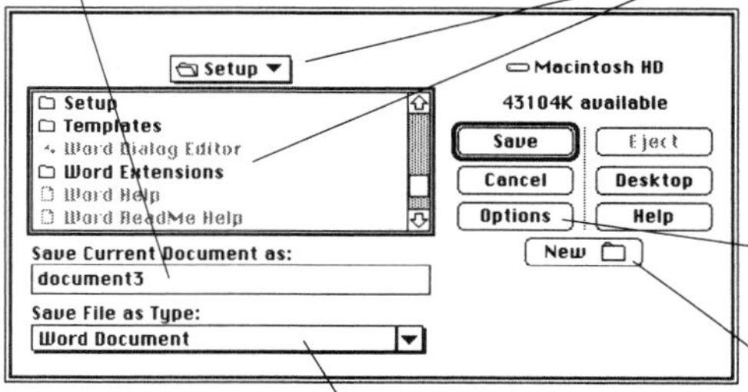

Type a name for the document here

Choose the folder to save the file in

Sets automatic save features

Creates a new folder for your document

Saves the document in a different file format

Figure 32 *Save As dialog box saves your new documents.*

Automatic Saving

Word comes configured to automatically save your documents every 10 minutes. While that may seem often enough, it means you risk loosing up to 10 minutes of work should there be a power failure. To change the auto save time period:

1 If the Save As dialog box is still open, click the Options button; otherwise, choose the Options command on the Tools menu **(Figure 33)**.

2 In the Options dialog box, click the Save tab if not already displayed **(Figure 34)**.

3 Click the **Automatic Save Every** option to add an **X**.

4 Now, enter a shorter time interval between each save in the Minutes box.

5 If you would like Word to automatically make a backup of each document, click the **Always Create Backup Copy** option to add an **X**.

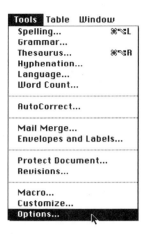

Figure 33 *Options command on the Tools menu.*

Click to always make a backup of your work

Click to add summaries to all new documents

Click to activate Auto Save

Enter a time interval between saves

Click to save changes to dialog box

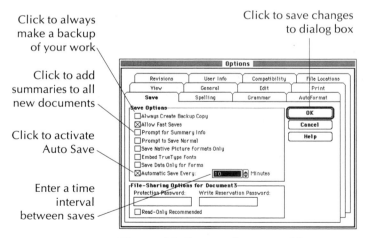

Figure 34 *Shorten the interval between auto saves with the Options dialog box.*

Figure 35 *Summary Info command on the File menu.*

Figure 36 *Summary Info dialog box records key information about your work.*

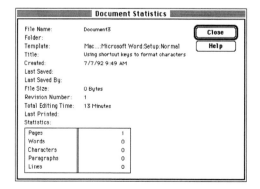

Figure 37 *Document Statistics dialog box.*

Document Summary

Now is a good time to fill out a summary of your newly saved document. Document summaries further define your work and give Word vital criteria to use in searching for your documents.

1 Open the File menu and choose the Summary Info command **(Figure 35)**.

2 You will see the Summary Info dialog box **(Figure 36)**. Fill in the appropriate information in the fields.

The keywords field holds search words that are key to the subject matter. The comments field can contain up to a 255-character description of the document.

3 To see a statistical summary of your document, click the **Statistics** button.

4 The Document Statistics dialog box **(Figure 37)** will open, with current information on your document.

Tip

■ If you would like to always fill out summary information on new documents, open the Options dialog box (see **Figure 34** on the previous page) and click the **Prompt for Summary** option to add an **X**. Now, whenever you save a document for the first time, the Summary Info dialog box will open automatically.

Zooming for a Better Look

If you need to get closer to your work, use the Zoom feature to find a comfortable magnification:

1   Choose the View menu **(Figure 38)** and select the Zoom command.

2   In the Zoom dialog box **(Figure 39)**, choose the percentage of magnification or reduction. To resize your document pages the width of the screen, choose the **Page Width** radio button.

3   Choose OK to return to your document. Your pages will be re-sized according to the percentage you specified in the dialog box.

4   For a faster zoom, use the **Zoom** button on the Standard toolbar **(Figure 40)**.

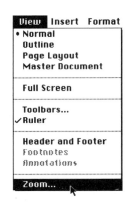

Figure 38 *Zoom command on the View menu.*

Current font and size selected

Preview of selected zoom

Click one of these buttons for preset views

Page Width spreads the text across the screen regardless of text size

This shows whole text plus margins

Enter the exact zoom percentage here between 20% and 200 %

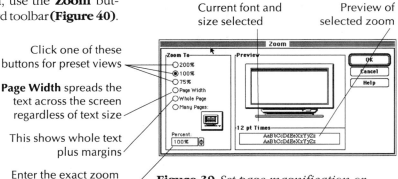

Figure 39 *Set page magnification or reduction with the Zoom dialog box.*

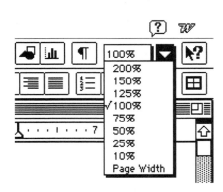

Figure 40 *A fast zoom using the Standard toolbar.*

The Zoom dialog box gives you a preview of the magnification or reduction you select:

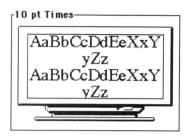

200% option

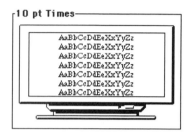

100% option

75% option

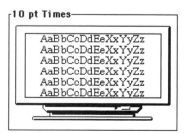

Page Width option

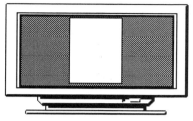

Choose Page Preview (on the File menu) and open the Zoom dialog box to click the **Whole Page** option

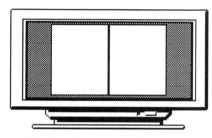

In Print Preview, choose the **Many Pages** option to view page spreads

In Page Preview, click the thumbnail picture button to see your document pages in thumbnail; click the page your zoom option will affect

Zooming

Moving Around

As you add text, Word scrolls the insertion point down the page to always keep it (and the text you're currently typing) visible in the document window. There are several ways to move through your document, each has its advantages depending on what you want to do:

- **Scroll bars**—move the pages up or down, without moving the insertion point **(Figure 41)**. In order to type in a new location after scrolling, you must first click the I-beam on the page where you want to type. Clicking the I-beam moves the insertion point. Shift the page left or right with the horizontal scroll bar.

- **Drag and Drop**—Once you drag an object to a new location, you can scroll the pages up or down by dragging off the bottom or top of the document window.

- **Keyboard**—Use the numeric cursor keys in combination with the Command key to move the insertion point through your document.

Click to scroll up (toward the beginning) in small steps

Click and drag the scroll box up or down, to move in large steps, toward the beginning or end

Click along the scrollbar to make the scroll box jump to the mouse pointer; the further you click from the arrows, the further you will scroll in your document

Click to scroll down (toward the end) in small steps

Figure 41 *Use the vertical scrollbar to move through your document.*

Beginning of line	Home
End of line	End
Beginning of paragraph	Cmd+Up arrow
End of paragraph	Cmd+Down arrow
Top of screen	Cmd+Page Up
Bottom of screen	Cmd+Page Down
Top of previous page	Cmd+Option+Page Up
Top of next page	Cmd+Option+Page Down
Beginning of document	Cmd+Home
End of document	Cmd+End

Tip

- Since the insertion point doesn't move when you scroll, if you want to move back instantly to the insertion point (without having to scroll back), simply type a character, or press one of the arrow keys on the keyboard. Word will jump back to the insertion point.

Format the Page

*O*_{NCE} you get your thoughts down in Word's document window, it's time to see how they can be arranged attractively on the pages you will eventually print. As you learned in the last chapter, Word understands formatting on a paragraph level—in fact, Word stores all the formatting options you choose in each paragraph of text. Press the Return key to begin a new paragraph and Word copies over the formatting from the previous paragraph. For simple page formats, set the format up in the first paragraph and Word will apply the format to all paragraph in your document.

For more sophisticated pages, you might want to add headers and footers, multiple columns, text within lined or shaded borders, figures and captions, or perhaps footnotes. As you will see in this chapter, Word can handle all these formatting requests with very little effort on your part.

Tip

▪ Word will show you a summary of each paragraph's formatting at any time. Simply click the question mark help button on the Standard toolbar, place the question mark pointer over any character in the paragraph and click. You'll see a summary of formatting, like this:

Paragraph Formatting
Paragraph Style: Indent: Left 0" Flush left
Direct:

Font Formatting
Paragraph Style: Font: Times, 10 pt, English (US)
Character Style:
Direct:

About Sections

Word uses sections to designate different page formats. Sections can be as short as a single paragraph, or many pages long. When you make formatting changes, Word creates a new section to hold the formats automatically. Section breaks separate sections **(Figure 1)**. In order to change from a single-column page to multiple columns, you must first create a new section to hold the different columns. Likewise, if you want to create different headers or footers for some pages, they must go in a new section. To create a new section:

1 Open the Insert menu and choose the Break command **(Figure 2)**.

2 In the Break dialog box **(Figure 3)**, choose the type of section you want.

3 To create a new section at the insertion point position, choose the **Continuous** radio button. To start a new page, with the new section at the beginning of the new page, choose **Next Page**.

4 Choose OK to return to your document.

5 To delete the section you created, place the insertion point immediately below the section break and press the Backspace key.

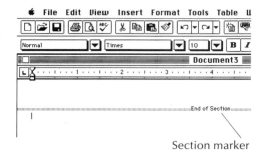

Section marker

Figure 1 *End-of-section marker shows break between sections.*

Figure 2 *Break command on the Insert menu.*

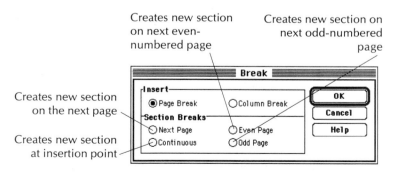

Creates new section on next even-numbered page

Creates new section on next odd-numbered page

Creates new section on the next page

Creates new section at insertion point

Figure 3 *Add new sections using the Break dialog box.*

Figure 4 *Document Layout command on the File menu.*

Figure 5 *Margins are set using the Document Layout dialog box.*

Figure 6 *Preview window shows mirrored margins.*

Figure 7 *Left and Right margins change to* Inside *and* Outside.

Defining the Page

The term *page* may have a different meaning to you than to Word. For example, there's the "page" that you type on, the page that is printed by your printer, or the physical piece of paper that moves through your printer. Word can define all of these pages and more. To set the page definition:

1 Click open the File menu and choose the Document Layout command **(Figure 4).**

2 In the Document Layout dialog box, click the Margins tab **(Figure 5)** to begin defining your pages.

3 Notice that as you change values in the margin text boxes, the preview example changes as well.

4 If you are planning to print on the front and back of your document pages (and bind the pages along the left edge like this book), click the **Mirror Margins** check box **(Figure 6)** to add an *X*. Notice that the preview changes to show two pages arranged like an open book, and the Left and Right margin boxes become *Inside* and *Outside* boxes **(Figure 7).**

5 Use the **Apply To** pop-up menu **(Figure 8)** to assign the margin values to all or part of the document. If you want to apply the values to only some text, highlight the text first and choose the **Highlighted Text** option. Word will place a section break immediately before the text you highlighted.

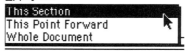

Figure 8 *Applying the margin settings.*

Defining Pages

Choosing the Paper Size

1 Choose the Page Setup command on the File menu to open the Page Setup dialog box **(Figure 9)**.

2 Choose the paper size that will be loaded into your printer. Use the **Paper Size** pop-up menu to pick a page size, or enter exact dimensions in the **Width** and **Height** text boxes.

3 Choose a paper **Orientation** (landscape or portrait).

4 Then, decide whether the paper size you specify here applies to all the pages of your document, or to a particular section or selected text. For instance, you might specify letter-size pages for a business letter, but specify an envelope for the last section.

5 If you want to make this paper size the default for new documents, click the **Default** button.

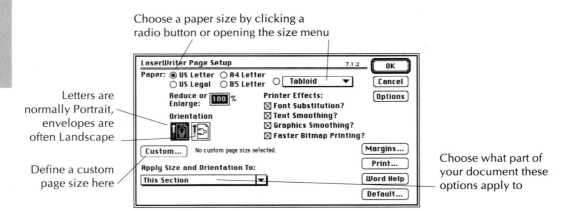

Choose a paper size by clicking a
radio button or opening the size menu

Letters are
normally Portrait,
envelopes are
often Landscape

Define a custom
page size here

Choose what part of
your document these
options apply to

Figure 9 *Use the Page Setup dialog box to choose
the overall page size for the printed document.*

Layout Decisions

1 Choose the Document Layout command on the File menu to open the Document Layout dialog box **(Figure 10)**.

2 Click open the **Section Start** pop-up menu and choose how you want sections to be added to your pages **(Figure 11)**.

3 Click the headers and footers check boxes to note how you want to control headers and footers.

4 Open the **Vertical Alignment** pop-up list **(Figure 12)** to set the top-to-bottom alignment of text on the page.

5 Finally, choose how you want these choices to apply to your document by clicking the **Apply To** pop-up menu.

Click **Section Start** and define how sections are to be added

Defines alternating headers and footers for odd and even pages

Defines a unique header and footer for first page of document

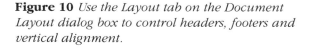

Figure 10 *Use the Layout tab on the Document Layout dialog box to control headers, footers and vertical alignment.*

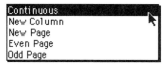

Figure 11 *Section Start pop-up menu offers choices for starting new sections in your document.*

Centers text on page

Evenly distributes paragraphs top to bottom on page

Figure 12 *Aligns paragraphs vertically on the page.*

Page Layout

About Tabs

Tabs are invisible markers you can use to align columns of information on the page **(Figure 13)**. They are set in Word much like they used to be set on a typewriter—remember? You positioned the tab stop along a ruler bar and when you pressed the tab key, the carriage would be released and slam into the tab stop.

In Word you use a similar (but much quieter) tab Ruler. Click the mouse arrow where you want to add a tab on the Ruler, press the Tab key and the insertion point will seek the next tab to the right.

While you may find it tempting to use the space bar to align text or numbers, what looks aligned will most certainly not print aligned. Use tabs to control alignment properly.

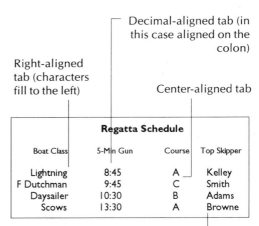

Figure 13 *Different tab alignments used in the same table.*

Setting Tabs using the Ruler

1 Select the text that will be affected by the new tab settings.

2 Click one of the four tab icons at the right edge of the Ruler **(Figure 14)**.

3 Now, move the mouse pointer onto the Ruler **(Figure 15)** and click where you want the tab added. To remove an existing tab, click and drag the tab marker off the Ruler.

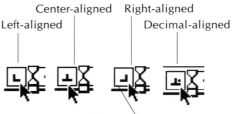

Figure 14 *Toolbar tab icons set tab alignment.*

Click the alignment you want, then click the position on the Ruler

Tip

■ Tab settings only affect text which follows the position of the text insertion point, or text which you have first selected. Word will copy the new settings to each new paragraph that you add.

Left-aligned tab marker

Figure 15 *The Ruler shows you all current tab positions.*

Tabs

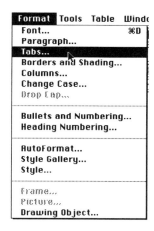

Figure 16 *Choose Tabs from the Format menu to open the Tabs dialog box.*

Setting Tabs using the Tabs Dialog Box

1 Choose the Tabs command from the Format menu **(Figure 16)**. Use the Tabs dialog box **(Figure 17)** to enter or remove tab positions and define the kind of tab you want.

2 For each tab you want to add, enter its position in the **Tab Stop Position** box.

3 Then choose the type of tab by clicking one of the **Alignment** buttons.

4 Assign a tab leader style if you want (leaders are characters, like repeating periods, that fill the space between tabs).

5 Click the **Set** button to save tab specifications and add the position to the position list.

6 Click OK to save the tab positions and return to your document.

Set evenly-spaced tabs by entering a default tab stop value

Enter exact tab positions here

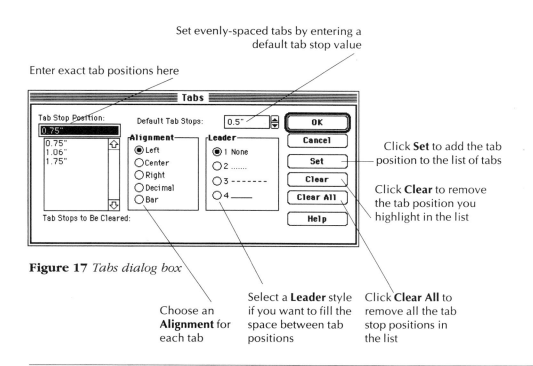

Click **Set** to add the tab position to the list of tabs

Click **Clear** to remove the tab position you highlight in the list

Figure 17 *Tabs dialog box*

Choose an **Alignment** for each tab

Select a **Leader** style if you want to fill the space between tab positions

Click **Clear All** to remove all the tab stop positions in the list

About Indents

Indents are different from tabs. Tabs are used to arrange tabular information—creating a time schedule is a very common use of tabs. Indents are used when you want to change the position of the left or right edges of a paragraph of text. Use the indent icons on the Ruler **(Figure 18)** to control indents.

Word gives you four types of indent choices:

- **First line left indent**, in which only the first line of a paragraph is indented.

- **Left edge indent**, which indents the left edge of all lines of the paragraph.

- **Hanging indent**, where the left edge of all but the first line are left indented.

- **Right edge indent**, where the right edge of all paragraph lines is indented.

Adding a First Line Indent

1 Click anywhere in the paragraph you want to indent.

2 Position the mouse pointer over the upper indent icon on the left side of the Ruler.

3 Click and drag the upper icon to the right, the amount of the indention. The first line of the paragraph will indent by the amount you specify **(Figure 19)**.

Adding a Left Edge Indent

1 Click anywhere in the paragraph you want to indent.

2 Click the bottom indent icon on the left edge of the ruler.

3 Drag the icon to the right the amount of the indention. Notice that the top icon will remain connected to the bottom icon and move with it **(Figure 20)**.

Controls **left indent** for all lines: Click and drag to the right to indent the left edge of the paragraph

Indents the first line: Click and drag to the right to indent just the first line

Controls **hanging indent**: indents all but the first line

Figure 18 *Left indent and hanging indent icons on the Ruler.*

Click and drag the top indent icon to the right

Sailing upwind, you could sense the boat struggling for a foothold in the ocean, and slipping to the lee as the seas built. Her shallow draft may have let her nose into many a

Figure 19 *Paragraph formatted with a first line left indent.*

Click and drag top and bottom indent icons

Sailing upwind, you could sense the boat struggling for a foothold in the ocean, and slipping to the lee as the seas built. Her shallow draft may have let her nose into many a thin lagoon in the islands, but

Figure 20 *Paragraph formatted with a left edge indent.*

Set Indents, First Line Indents

Drag the top indent icon back to the original position to outdent the first line

Drag the bottom indent icon to the right to indent the remaining lines

Sailing upwind, you could sense the boat struggling for a foothold in the ocean, and slipping to the lee as the seas built. Her shallow draft may have let her nose into many a thin lagoon in the islands, but

Figure 21 *Paragraph formatted with a hanging indent.*

Indents the right edge of the paragraph: Click and drag to the left to indent

Figure 22 *Right indent icon on the Ruler.*

Right edge indent icon creates the indent

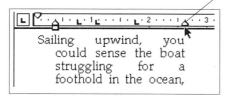

Sailing upwind, you could sense the boat struggling for a foothold in the ocean,

Figure 23 *Paragraph formatted with a right edge indent.*

Adding a Hanging Indent

1 Click anywhere in the paragraph you want to indent.

2 Click the bottom indent icon and drag it to the right the amount of the indention. The top indent icon will move with the bottom indent icon.

3 Now, click the top indent icon and drag it back to the left to create the hanging indent—the paragraph "hangs" under the first line **(Figure 21)**.

Tip

■ You can also create numbered or bulletted hanging indent **lists** using the indent buttons on the toolbar. See Chapter 8.

Adding a Right Edge Indent

1 Click anywhere in the paragraph you want to indent.

2 Click the right indent icon **(Figure 22)** and drag it to the left the amount of the indention. The right edge of each paragraph line will indent **(Figure 23)**.

Tip

■ To use your indent or tab settings in other documents, save the paragraphs containing the settings as a style. See Chapter 9.

Hanging Indents, Right Edge Indents

Setting Borders

Borders are lines that are added to surround paragraphs. Word gives you the options of boxing paragraphs, or simply adding lines above, below, or to each side. To set borders:

1 Choose the Borders and Shading command on the Format menu **(Figure 24)**.

2 In the Paragraph Borders and Shading dialog box **(Figure 25)**, click one of the **Preset** borders or use the borders preview model to create a custom border.

3 Use the **From Text** pop-up menu to set the border standoff (how far the border is placed from the text it surrounds).

4 Choose a style of border line from the **Style** menu and a color from the **Color** menu.

5 To delete an existing border, choose the **None** radio button.

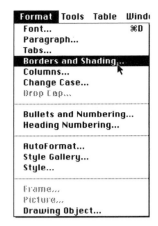

Figure 24 *Borders and Shading command on the Format menu.*

Chooses a preset box or drop shadow style

Click either to turn off borders

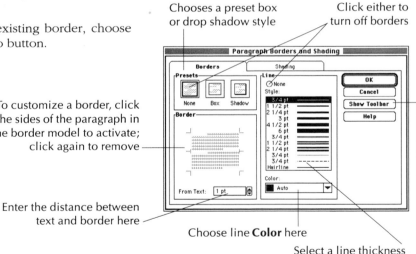

To customize a border, click the sides of the paragraph in the border model to activate; click again to remove

Enter the distance between text and border here

Choose line **Color** here

Select a line thickness

Figure 25 *Define borders around paragraphs with the Paragraph Borders and Shading dialog box.*

Click to display the Borders toolbar

Borders

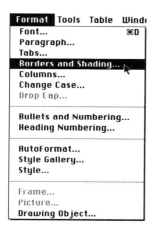

Figure 26 *Borders and Shading command on the Format menu.*

Setting Shading

Shading adds a background shade or color behind text and graphics. To set the degree of shading or color:

1 Choose the Borders and Shading command on the Format menu **(Figure 26)**.

2 Click the Shading tab in the Paragraph Borders and Shading dialog box **(Figure 27)**.

3 Choose the percentage of shade from the **Shading** menu.

4 To delete existing shading, choose the **None** radio button.

Tips

■ To create reversed type out of a black background, choose Solid as the shading. Then choose the Font command on the Format menu to open the Font dialog box and set the text color to White.

■ Use the Table AutoFormat command button (on the Insert Table dialog box) to add borders to tables. See Chapter 10 for details.

Click **None** to turn off shading

Click the percentage of shading up to solid (100%)

Foreground normally means the color of dots on a white background

Preview window shows your shading choice

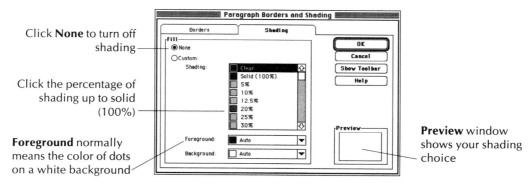

Figure 27 *Click the Shading tab in the Paragraph and Shading dialog box to define background shading.*

Formatting Paragraphs

1 Choose the Paragraph command on the Format menu **(Figure 28)**. You will see the Paragraph dialog box **(Figure 29)**.

2 Set up paragraph indents by entering values in the **Left** or **Right** boxes.

3 Open the **Special** pop-up menu to select either first line or hanging indents and add the amount of indent in the **By** text box.

4 Add extra line space before or after paragraphs by entering a measurement value in the **Before** or **After** text boxes. Note that if you choose both before and after spacing, you will have double the amount of space between paragraphs.

5 Set paragraph alignment in the **Alignment** menu.

6 Set the amount of line spacing in the **Line Spacing** text box.

Tip

■ To establish line leading for your text, choose Exact from the Line Spacing menu and enter the number of points of leading you want in the At box. Leading is usually 120 percent of the type size (10 point type should have about 12 points of leading).

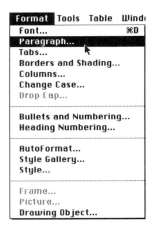

Figure 28 *Paragraph command on the Format menu.*

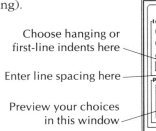
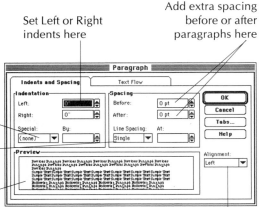

Set Left or Right indents here

Add extra spacing before or after paragraphs here

Choose hanging or first-line indents here

Enter line spacing here

Preview your choices in this window

Set paragraph alignment (left-aligned, centered, right-aligned or justified)

Figure 29 *Make paragraph formatting choices in the Paragraph dialog box.*

Paragraphs

Page header

Figure 30 *Example of page header and footer.*

Page footer

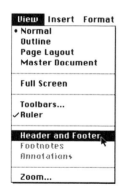

Figure 31 *Header and Footer command on the View menu.*

Adding Headers and Footers

Headers and footers repeat text or graphics at the top or bottom (respectively) of your pages **(Figure 30)**. Page numbers are the most common header or footer, but virtually anything can be in headers or footers. To create headers and footers:

1 Choose the Header and Footer command on the View menu **(Figure 31)**.

2 The page will dim and you will see a header area above the top margin **(Figure 32)**. Use the Header and Footer toolbar to create the header or footer you want.

3 Click the Switch Between Header and Footer button to display the footer area below the bottom margin; click the button again to move back to the header. Type what you want in the header and footer areas.

4 Now, use the formatting toolbar to format the text.

5 To create page numbers in the header or footer, click the page number button on the Header and Footer toolbar. Likewise, click the date and time buttons to add the current date and time to the header or footer.

Tip

■ Once you have created a header or footer, you can open it by clicking the dimmed text in the document window.

Headers and Footers

Same as previous header or footer

Move to next or previous header or footer

Add page number, date, or time

Click to switch between header and footer

Click to close and return to your document

Header and Footer

Close

Page Setup dialog box

Figure 32 *Header and Footer toolbar.*

Alternating Headers and Footers

Word can handle different headers or footers on either odd or even pages. Called *alternating* headers or footers, they are like the headers in this book: odd pages carry the chapter title; even pages carry the chapter number. To set up alternating even and odd page headers or footers:

1 Click the Document Layout button on the Headers and Footers toolbar.

2 In the Document Layout dialog box **(Figure 33)**, click the **Different Odd and Even** check box to add an X. Choose OK to close the dialog box.

3 Then, in the header or footer area, Word will label the current header or footer as either odd or even **(Figure 34)**. To set up the second header or footer, click the Show Next button.

4 When you've finished entering the second header or footer, click **Close** to return to your document. The headers will be dimmed, but visible.

Click to create odd and even page headers or footers

Figure 33 *Layout tab on Document layout dialog box defines odd/even headers and footers.*

Word tells you whether this is an odd or even page header

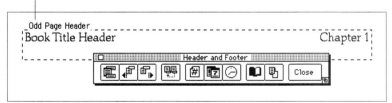

Figure 34 *The header or footer area is labeled to show odd or even pages.*

First Page Headers or Footers

Sometimes it's nice to have a different header or footer on the first page of a document. Here are the steps:

1 Move to the first page of your document and choose the Header and Footer command on the View menu.

 2 Click the Document Layout button to open the Document Layout dialog box **(Figure 35)**.

3 Click the **Different First Page** check box to add an X.

4 Click OK to return to your header or footer. Now, create the different header or footer for the first page of your document.

5 When you are through with the first header or footer, click the Show Next button to create the second header or footer that will be used for the remainder of your document pages.

6 Now create the second header or footer and click **Close** to return to your document.

Click to create a different first page header or footer

Figure 35 *Layout tab on the Page Setup dialog box defines first page headers and footers.*

Headers and Footers

Adding Columns

1 Choose the Columns command on the Format menu **(Figure 36)** to open the Columns dialog box **(Figure 37)**.

2 Pick one of the preset column configurations, or enter the number of columns you want in the **Number of Columns** box. Word will calculate the column width and spacing and display the results in the **Width** and **Spacing** boxes.

3 Add a line between each column by clicking the **Line Between** check box.

4 Choose OK to save the column definition and return to your document.

Tips

■ For a quick, simple column setup, click the Columns button on the standard toolbar **(Figure 38)**. Drag the pointer across the number of columns you want and release. The columns will be added at the insertion point position.

■ If you want to use columns to align text or figures, you may find it easier to create a table (see Chapter 10).

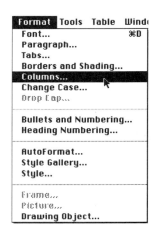

Figure 36 *Columns command on the Format menu.*

Choose one of the preset definitions

Or, enter the number of columns

Word calculates spacing, but to modify, enter your own values here

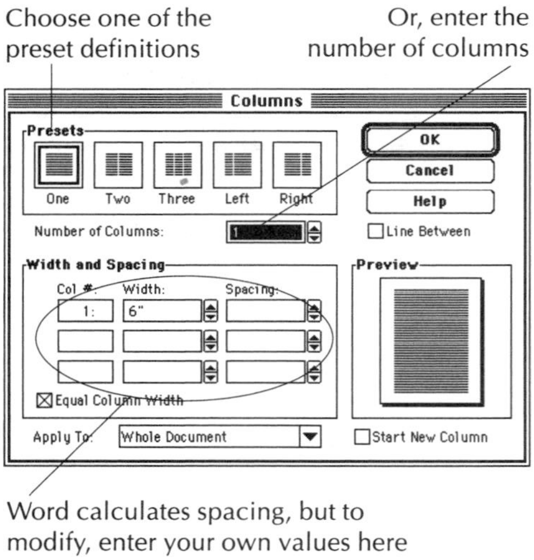

Figure 37 *Columns dialog box.*

Click to create columns

2 Columns

Figure 38 *Standard toolbar columns button quickly defines up to four evenly-spaced columns.*

Print It

*W*ᴏʀᴅ will print your document quickly and efficiently with little, if any fuss or bother. And, these days there's such a rich palette of printers at your disposal: From the LaserWriter Plus, to a wide range of laser and color printers from Hewlett-Packard, to die sublimation printers from QMS to very high resolution laser printers from NewGen, LaserMaster and Xante.

Regardless of the actual hardware, it's a simple matter to select the exact printer you need from the Chooser and click the Printer icon on Word's toolbar. When the crisp, clean look of typesetting is called for, it's just as simple to save your Word document to file and pack it off to a service bureau where gorgeous pages will form like magic on a PostScript imagesetter like the Linotronic L-630 or the Agfa SelectSet 5000.

And, while Word can print the pages of your documents, it can just as easily handle your envelopes as well as odd page sizes for booklets, brochures, business cards, folders, and much more.

Introduction

Previewing Pages

You're ready to print, but let's first get a bird's eye view of what the page will look like. Even though Word is a WYSIWYG word processor—what you see in the document window is the same as what you see on the printed page—the Print Preview command let's you see the whole page exactly as it will be printed.

1 Choose the Print Preview command on the File menu **(Figure 1)**.

2 You will see the Print Preview window **(Figure 2)**. While you can't type, you can many of the menu commands while you're in the preview window.

3 Use the Preview toolbar **(Figure 3)** to view your work from different magnifications and display different pages.

4 Click the Full button to see a full screen view of the page **(Figure 4)**.

5 Choose Close to return to the document window.

Page Preview

File	Edit	View	Inser
New...			⌘N
Open...			⌘O
Close			⌘W
Save			⌘S
Save As...			
Save All			
Find File...			
Summary Info...			
Templates...			
Document Layout...			
Page Setup...			
Print Preview			
Print...			⌘P
Quit			⌘Q

Figure 1 *Print Preview command on the File menu.*

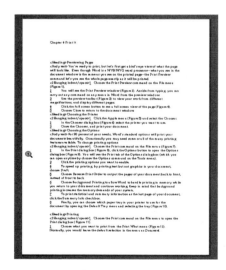

Figure 2 *Print Preview shows a bird's eye view of the page.*

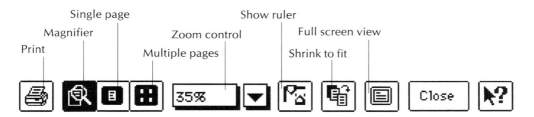

Figure 3 *Print Preview toolbar.*

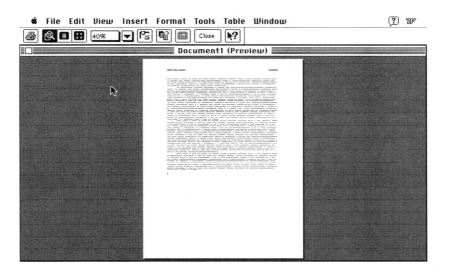

Figure 4 *Print Preview full screen view.*

Page Preview

Choosing the Printer

Word will print to whatever printer is currently selected. If you use color in your document, you must choose a color printer to print the colors. To select the printer:

1 Click the Apple menu **(Figure 5)** and select the Chooser.

2 In the Chooser dialog box **(Figure 6)** select the printer you want to use. Click the **Active** button to make AppleTalk active and activate background printing by choose the **On** radio button.

3 Close the Chooser, decide what printing options you want and print your document.

Figure 5 *Apple menu.*

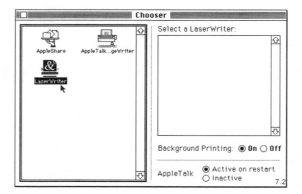

Figure 6 *Select the active printer in the Chooser dialog box.*

Printer Selection

Figure 7 *Print command on the File menu.*

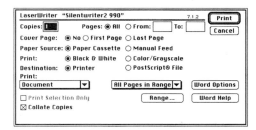

Figure 8 *Print dialog box.*

Choosing Printer Options

For 90 percent of your needs, Word's standard options will print your documents beautifully. Occasionally you may need some or all of the many printing features available. To change printing options:

1 Choose the Print command on the File menu **(Figure 7)**.

2 In the Print dialog box **(Figure 8)**, click the **Word Options** button to open the Options dialog box **(Figure 9)**. You will see the Print tab of the Options dialog box (which you can open anytime by choosing the Options command on the Tools menu).

3 Click the printing options you want to enable.

To print statistical and summary information as the last page of your document, click the **Summary Info** check box

Choose **Reverse Print Order** to output the pages of your document back to front, instead of front to back

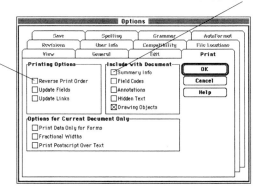

Figure 9 *Print tab on the Options dialog box lets you further define printing.*

Printer Options

Printing

1. Choose the Print command on the File menu **(Figure 10)** to open the Print dialog box **(Figure 11)**.
2. Define what pages of your document you want to print and in what order they will print.
3. Click OK to start printing.

Tip

- You can print on the front and back of your pages, creating two-sided documents, by using the Print menu. First, choose **Odd Pages**. When they have printed, turn them over, put them back in your printer's paper tray and choose **Even Pages**.

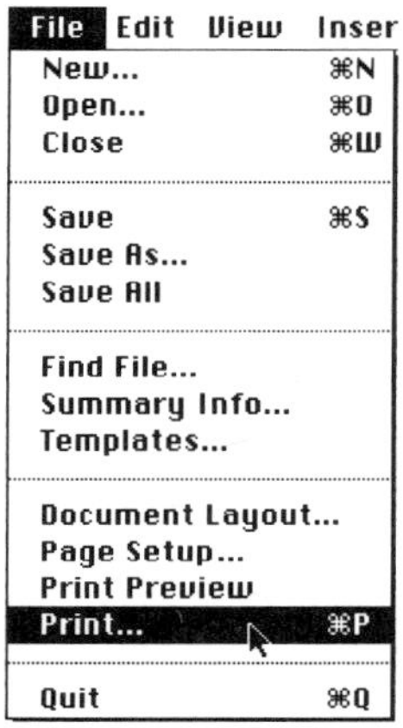

Figure 10 *Print command on the File menu.*

Choose **Print** to begin printing

Enter the number of copies to be printed in the **Copies** text box

In the **Print** menu, choose the order of printing pages you have specified in the Print Range (you can choose to print the pages in order, or print either odd or even pages first)

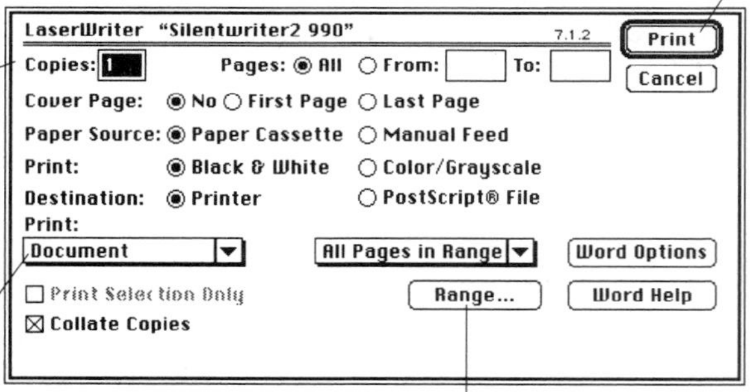

Figure 11 *Print dialog box.*

Enter the **Page Range** for the number of pages you want printed—you can enter a range of pages by typing individual page numbers separated by commas (2,3,4,5,6) or enter a range of pages (2-6)

File	Edit	View	Inser
New...			⌘N
Open...			⌘O
Close			⌘W
Save			⌘S
Save As...			
Save All			
Find File...			
Summary Info...			
Templates...			
Document Layout...			
Page Setup...			
Print Preview			
Print...			⌘P
Quit			⌘Q

Figure 12 *Page Setup command on the File menu.*

Controlling Paper Size

If your printer has two paper trays, or one tray and a manual feed slot, you can handle different sizes of paper for different printing situations. Here's how to set paper sizes:

1 Choose the Page Setup command on the File menu **(Figure 12)** to open the Page Setup dialog box, to open the Page Setup dialog box **(Figure 13)**. Note that the dialog box is specific to the kind of printer you've selected with the Chooser).

2 Choose the paper size by clicking the appropriate radio button. To print subsequent pages on different size paper, position the insertion point where you want a paper size change, choose the new size, and select **This Point Forward** in the Apply Size and Orientation To menu.

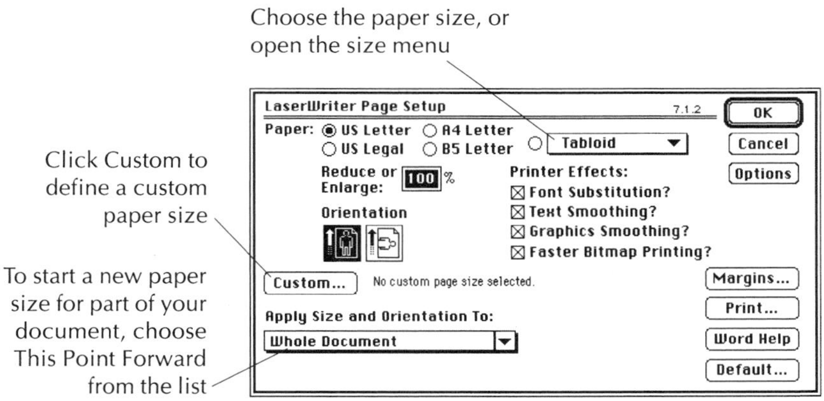

Choose the paper size, or open the size menu

Click Custom to define a custom paper size

To start a new paper size for part of your document, choose This Point Forward from the list

LaserWriter Page Setup   7.1.2   [OK]

Paper: ⦿ US Letter ○ A4 Letter
       ○ US Legal   ○ B5 Letter ○ [Tabloid ▼]   [Cancel]   [Options]

Reduce or [100]%   Printer Effects:
Enlarge: ☒ Font Substitution?
Orientation   ☒ Text Smoothing?
                    ☒ Graphics Smoothing?
                    ☒ Faster Bitmap Printing?

[Custom...] No custom page size selected.   [Margins...]
                                                [Print...]
Apply Size and Orientation To:
[Whole Document   ▼]   [Word Help]
                                                [Default...]

Figure 13 *Page Setup dialog box defines preset and custom paper sizes.*

Printing: Paper Source

3 Now choose the tray for the remaining pages from the **Other Pages** menu.

Using Service Bureaus

You printer will be fine for many of the documents you will produce with Word. Yet sometimes you may need the professional look of high-resolution typesetting. When the job must look its best, you can print your document to disk and send it to a PostScript service bureau for high-resolution printing.

Printing to disk means a copy of the document is saved on your computer's disk drive in the machine language of bits and bytes that the printing device understands. Then the service bureau, which owns an expensive imagesetter, can download the machine-language file directly to the printer to be printed. Follow these steps:

Printing to Disk

1 Click open the Apple menu and select the Chooser **(Figure 14)**. Now click on the PostScript printer driver (the LaserWriter printer driver will work just fine).

2 Choose the Print command on the File menu **(Figure 15)** to open the Print dialog box **(Figure 16)**.

3 Click the **Print PostScript** option.

4 Now, choose OK. You will see the Print to File dialog box **(Figure 17)**. Enter a file name for this document. Usually, documents destined for service bureau output are named with the extension *.PS* to indicate it is a PostScript file.

5 Choose OK to write out the file to your hard or floppy disk.

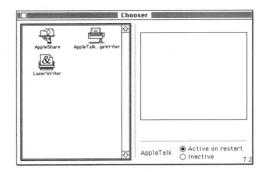

Figure 14 *Select the printer you want to use in the Chooser dialog box.*

Figure 15 *Print command on the File menu.*

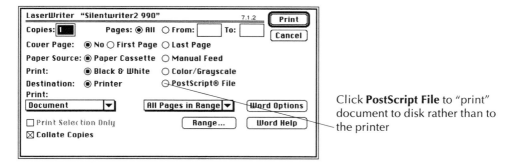

Click **PostScript File** to "print" document to disk rather than to the printer

Figure 16 *Print dialog box can control printing to file as well as to your printer.*

Enter name for print-to-disk file (add .PS to the end of the file name)

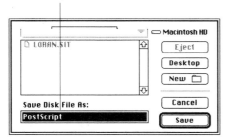

Figure 17 *Enter the name of the file in the Print to File dialog box.*

About Envelopes

Nothing used to be more trouble than adjusting, aligning and coercing addresses on labels and envelopes. Nothing is easier in Word. Whether it is a single envelope to go with a letter, or sheets of Avery labels for addresses, file folders, and floppy disks, Word has a dialog box that handles the work quickly and efficiently.

One note of caution: if you intend to print labels and envelopes with a laser printer, it should have a straight-through paper path. Older laser printers tended to turn the paper 180 degrees, which can jam envelopes and cause labels to peel and stick in places that only a technician with a three-digit hourly rate can reach. Likewise, you should be sure that the adhesive used on labels and envelopes can withstand the heat of the printer's fusing element. Check the technical manual to be sure.

Printing Envelopes

1 Type a letter in Word as you normally would **(Figure 18)**. When finished, choose the Envelopes and Labels command on the Tools menu **(Figure 19)** to open the Envelopes and Labels dialog box **(Figure 20)**.

2 Notice that Word has pulled the name and address from your letter and added them to the Delivery Address box. Change the information in the box if you want.

3 Word gets the information in the Return Address block from the User Information tab in the Options dialog box (on the Tools menu). You can change the return address information if you want, or omit it for preprinted envelopes by clicking the Omit check box.

August 4, 1994

Mr. Sam Lee
President
AllSoft Computer Software, Inc.
1 AllSoft Drive
Tampa, FL 32894

Dear Sam:

Thank you for your warm hospitality during my visit last week, and the beautiful cruise on Tampa Bay. I feel certain we can bring these negotiations to a successful conclusion, beneficial to both our companies. I'll call next week to bring over the backup material you requested.

Best regards,

Sid Bradley
Bradley Programming Services

Figure 18 *Word can automatically pull the name and address block from a business letter to create the envelope.*

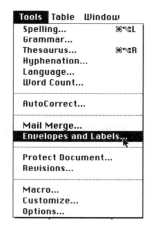

Figure 19 *Envelopes and Labels command on the Tools menu.*

Envelopes

4 Choose the Add to Document button to add the envelope configuration as the first section of your letter **(Figure 21)**, or click Print to immediately print the envelope.

Word pulls the name and address from the letter and adds them to the **Delivery Address** box

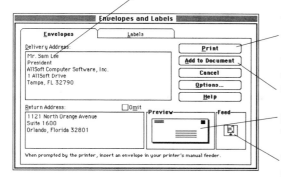

To print the envelope immediately, click **Print**

To add the envelope text as a new first section to your letter, Click **Add to Document**

Preview shows what your envelope will look like

The **Feed** icon shows you how to feed the envelope into the printer

Figure 20 *Envelopes tab on the Envelopes and Labels dialog box configures envelopes and prints them.*

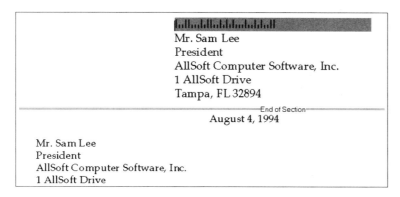

Figure 21 *Formatted envelope text (in this case, with barcode) is added as a beginning section to letter when you select **Add to Document** in the Envelopes and Labels dialog box.*

Envelopes

Formatting Envelopes

Out of the box, Word is set up to print number 10 business envelopes, in a specific typeface and size. But the application can print many sizes of envelopes, formatted exactly the way you want them.

1 Choose the Envelopes and Labels command on the Tools menu **(Figure 22)**.

2 In the Envelopes and Labels dialog box, click the **Options** button to open the Envelope Options dialog box **(Figure 23)**.

3 Choose a preset size from the Size menu or select Custom size and enter the exact dimensions. Note, that the envelope can be no larger than the maximum paper size your printer can accept.

4 To change the font for the delivery or return address, click the appropriate **Font** button. You will see the Font dialog box. When you are finished specifying the font, choose OK to return to the Envelope Options dialog box.

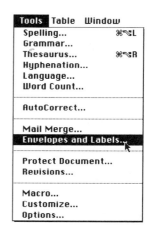

Figure 22 *Envelopes and Labels command on the Tools menu.*

Choose the **Envelope Size** from the pop-up menu

Click to add zip code barcodes

Click the **Font** buttons to change font and type size for the delivery and return addresses

These change the position of the address blocks on the envelope

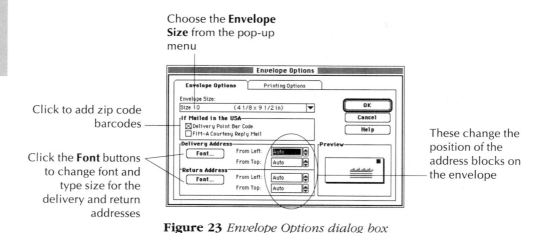

Figure 23 *Envelope Options dialog box lets you customize envelope printing.*

Add Graphics

GRAPHICS are anything you add to your pages besides text: clipart from Word's clipart library, drawings or paintings you create in a draw or paint program, illustrations from Adobe illustrator or Aldus FreeHand; even photos from Kodak Photo CDs. Word recognizes a wide variety of graphic formats, including PICT and PICT2, TIFF, EPSF, Paint bitmaps (PNTG),Windows metafiles, and WordPerfect graphic files.

The integration of text and graphics on Word's pages has never been easier. Word can treat the graphic as another character on the page, or, if added in a frame, as a totally independent object. Graphics can be pasted from other applications, or interactively linked to the applications that created them.

Introduction

Importing Graphics

1 Position the text insertion point where you want to add the graphic. Then choose the Picture command on the Insert menu **(Figure 1)** to open the Insert Picture dialog box **(Figure 2)**.

2 Find the graphic you want to insert. Open the **List Files of Type** menu to choose the correct import filter for the graphic you want.

3 To see a preview of each graphic, click the **Preview** check box.

4 Click OK to insert the graphic at the insertion point position.

Tips

▪ If you lack an import filter for the type of graphic you want to import, open the graphic in another application and copy it to the Clipboard. Then, in Word, paste the graphic from the Clipboard. Word will automatically convert the graphic to a type it does recognize.

▪ To speed up inserting a graphic, turn off the preview feature in the Picture dialog box by clicking the **Preview** check box to remove the X.

Figure 1 *Picture command on the Insert menu.*

Click **Insert** to add the graphic to your document at the insertion point position

Find the graphic file you want to import

Or, click open the **List Files of Type** menu to choose a specific graphic format

Click **Preview Picture** to see a small rendering of each graphic you choose in the file name list

Figure 2 *Use the Insert Picture dialog box to find and import graphics.*

Figure 3 *Sizing handles appear when you click the graphic.*

Figure 4 *Graphic enlarged proportionally using the sizing handles.*

Sizing Graphics

Once a graphic is inserted, you can resize it or trim away *(crop)* portions you don't want.

1 Click .to highlight the graphic. You will see the sizing handles **(Figure 3)**.

2 To resize the graphic proportionally, click and drag one of the corner handles to enlarge or shrink the graphic. As you drag, you will see a dashed line indicating the changing size; notice that the width and height change proportionally **(Figure 4)**.

3 To crop the image, hold down the Shift key and click and drag a handle in or out **(Figure 5)**.

4 To remove the graphic, click to highlight and press the Delete key.

Tip

■ To undo a sizing change, open the Format menu and choose Picture. Then click the **Reset** button.

Cropping icon

Figure 5 *Shift+click a sizing handle to crop away portions of the graphic.*

Wrapping Text Around Graphics

When you insert a graphic onto the page, it rests on an invisible line of type, much like an enlarged character of type. In order for lines of type to wrap around the graphic you must add it to a frame. Follow these steps:

1 Choose the Frame command on the Insert menu **(Figure 6)**.

2 The insertion point will change to an alignment crosshairs. Click and drag from the imaginary upper left corner down and to the right—as you drag you'll see a dashed line indicating the respective size of the frame. Release the mouse button when the frame is the size you want **(Figure 7)**.

3 If you have already added a graphic to your page, click and drag the graphic into the frame. Word will automatically proportionally resize the graphic to fit the frame.

4 To wrap text around the framed graphic, click the frame to highlight and choose the Frame command on the Format menu **(Figure 8)**.

5 In the Frame dialog box **(Figure 9)**, choose the **Around** icon button.

Tip

■ You can adjust the distance between text that is wrapped around a graphic and the edge of the graphic (called the *standoff*) by using the **Distance From** Text box. Enter a larger value to increase the amount of standoff; a smaller value will reduce the standoff.

Figure 6 *Frame command on the Insert menu.*

Figure 7 *Frame indicated by the shaded line.*

Graphics in Frames

Figure 8 *Frame command on the Format menu.*

To wrap text, choose the **Around** text wrapping button

To set an exact position for the frame, fill in the **Horizontal** and **Vertical** position

Adjust standoff (space between text and graphic) by filling in **Distance from Text** boxes

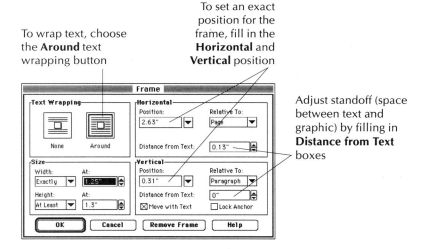

Figure 9 *Use the Frame dialog box to set text to wrap around the frame and graphic.*

Modifying Graphics

Once a graphic is added to your page, simply double-click it to open the graphic editor and display the Drawing toolbar **(Figure 10)**.

1. Choose the **Text Box** button to add a text box to the graphic **(Figure 11)**.
2. To define and add lines to the graphic, click the **Line** button **(Figure 12)**.
3. To modify the color of an object, click the **Fill** button **(Figure 13)**.
4. To close the editor, click the **Close** button on the Picture toolbar.

Tip

- You can click the drawing button on the Standard toolbar at any time to display the Drawing toolbar and add a drawing to the pages of your document.

Picture in Setup:document1
Picture
Close Picture
Drawing

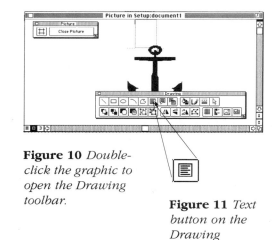

Figure 10 *Double-click the graphic to open the Drawing toolbar.*

Figure 11 *Text button on the Drawing Toolbar.*

More...
Select the line style on the menu, or click **More** to see more definitions

Figure 12 *Line button in the Drawing toolbar defines lines.*

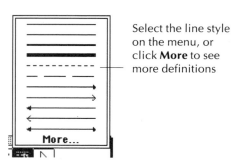

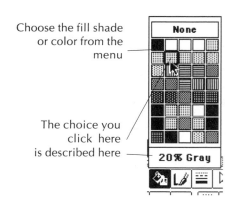

Choose the fill shade or color from the menu
The choice you click here is described here
None
20% Gray

Figure 13 *Fill button defines the fill color.*

Adding Callouts

Callouts annotate graphics: an arrow or line points out a pertinent detail and a brief text description adds information about that detail. To add a callout to your graphic:

1 Double-click the graphic to open the graphic editor and the Drawing toolbar.

2 Click the **Format Callout** button to display the Callout Defaults dialog box **(Figure 14)**. Define the style of callout you want for this document.

3 Now, click the **Callout** button. The insertion point will change to a crosshairs icon. Click the crosshairs where you want to begin the callout and drag off the graphic. Enter the text for the callout in the callout box.

Choose the **Type** of callout for your illustration

Gap is distance between line and text

Choose Any **Angle** to have Word adjust automatically

Drop is the location of the callout line and the text; enter a value or choose **Top**, **Center** or **Bottom**

Format callout button opens the dialog box

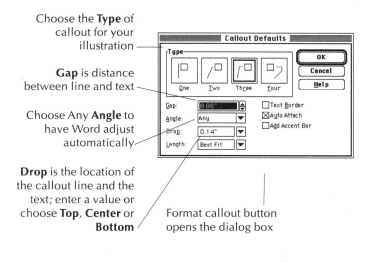

Figure 14 *Define callouts with the Callout Defaults dialog box.*

Checking Import Filters

If you open the Insert Picture dialog box to add a graphic, and you don't see the graphic type you want in the List Files of Type pop-up menu, you will have to load the import filter. To see a list of currently installed filters:

1 Choose About Word from the Apple menu **(Figure 15)**.

2 In the title and copyright window, click System Info to see a list of the installed import and export filters **(Figure 16)**.

3 To add or delete filters, quit Word, open the Microsoft Word Setup folder, and double-click on the Microsoft Word Setup program icon.

Figure 15 *About Microsoft Word command on the Apple menu.*

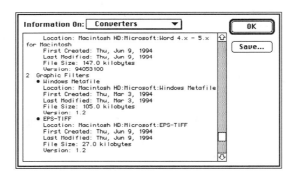

Figure 16 *System Info dialog box shows list of Converters (import and export filters) for graphic formats.*

Typography

*I*_F you're new to the Macintosh, you might be asking yourself what's a chapter on typography doing in a book about word processing. Typography is the act of using specific typefaces, in specific styles and sizes, to elicit a particular response—all of which you can do easily in Word. In fact, Word controls the kerning and leading of type, modifies type fonts to add expression and interest to your words; even lets you add an artistic flare with a clever program called WordArt. Word can even handle large initial characters (like the large initial *I* that kicks off this paragraph). Whether you're working with Adobe Type-1 fonts or TrueType fonts, Word can make your documents more attractive, by picking just the right typeface, with the perfect amount of spacing.

Handling Space on the Page

Space can be defined in many different ways. Traditional word processors, Word included, define space as a measure of line spacing—single spacing, space-and-a-half, double or triple spacing. Line spacing is a carry-over from how space was set on a typewriter. In typography, the size of space—called *leading* (rhymes with bedding)—is defined in points, just as the size of type is defined. In Word, you can set line spacing if you like, or specify leading in points. To change space or leading:

1 Highlight the paragraphs you want the spacing change to affect.

2 Choose the Paragraph command on the Format menu **(Figure 1)**. You will see the Paragraph dialog box **(Figure 2)**.

3 In the Indents and Spacing tab, click open the **Line Spacing** pop-up menu **(Figure 3)** and choose the type of spacing. For more than double-spacing, choose **Multiple** and enter the number of lines (for example, 3 for triple spacing) in the **At** box.

Tips

■ The usual amount of leading for text is about 120 percent of the type size. So, if the text is set in 11 point type, you would click **Exactly** on the Line Spacing menu, and enter 13.2 in the **At** box.

■ Here's a quick shortcut for setting line spacing: press **Cmd+1** to set single spacing, **Cmd+5** to set 1.5 line spacing, or **Cmd+2** for double spacing.

Figure 1 *Paragraph command on the Format menu.*

Open **Line Spacing** and choose the option for your document

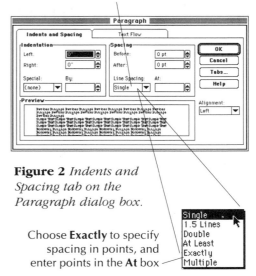

Figure 2 *Indents and Spacing tab on the Paragraph dialog box.*

Choose **Exactly** to specify spacing in points, and enter points in the **At** box

Figure 3 *Line Spacing menu.*

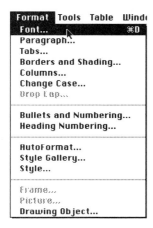

Figure 4 *Font command on the Format menu.*

Changing Character Spacing

Each character needs a bit of space around it to separate it from its neighbors. Normally, Word uses the default character spacing intended by the font's designer. Yet Word can stretch or compress space to suit the needs of your design. To change character spacing:

1 Highlight the text you want to expand or condense.

2 Choose the Font command on the Format menu **(Figure 4)** to open the Font dialog box.

3 Now, click the Character Spacing tab **(Figure 5)**.

4 To stretch the spacing, open the **Spacing** menu and choose **Expand**; choose **Condense** to compress character spacing. Enter the amount you wish to expand or condense in the **By** box. The results are displayed in the Preview box **(Figure 6)**.

Open the **Spacing** menu and choose **Expand** or **Condense**

Then enter the amount to expand or condense

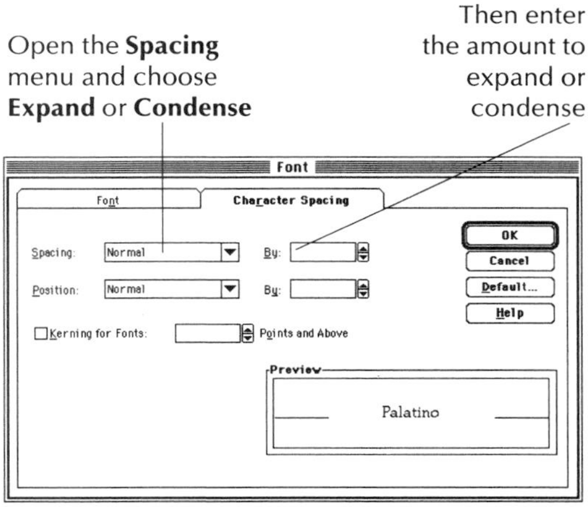

Figure 5 *Character Spacing tab on the Font dialog box controls expanding or condensing space between characters.*

Figure 6 *As you modify spacing, the Preview box displays the changes (shown here with expanded spacing).*

Changing Character Spacing

Shifting the Character Baseline

All characters rest on an invisible line, called the *baseline* **(Figure 7)**. Baselines are much like the lines of a writing tablet—they keep the characters of words even and attractive. Sometimes you may want to shift the baseline of one or more characters up or down. Follow these steps:

1 Highlight the characters whose baselines you want to shift.

2 Choose the Font command on the Format menu to open the Font dialog box.

3 Now click on the Character Spacing tab **(Figure 8)**.

4 Open the **Position** pop-up menu and select either **Raised** or **Lowered**. Then enter the amount you want to raise or lower the baseline in the **By** box.

Shifting the baseline can create interesting visual effects **(Figure 9)**.

Tip

▪ Superscripting or subscripting characters (which you select from the list of effects on the Font tab) simply shifts the baseline up or down by a set amount. An easy shortcut is to press Cmd++ for superscript, or Cmd+= for subscript.

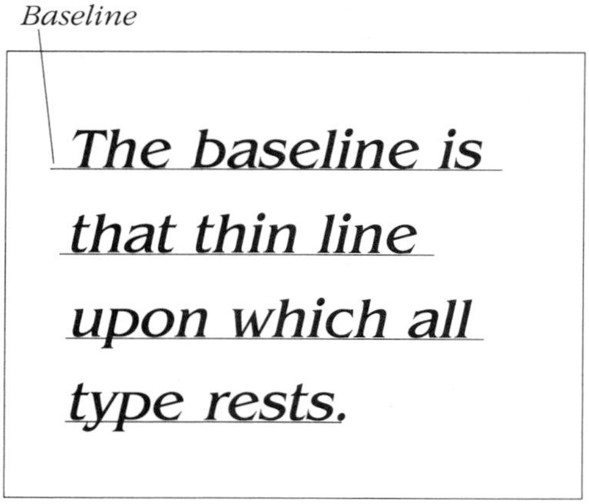

Baseline

The baseline is that thin line upon which all type rests.

Figure 7 *Type "rests" on its invisible baseline (shown for illustration only).*

Open the **Position** menu to raise or lower the baseline

Enter the amount of baseline shift in the **By** box

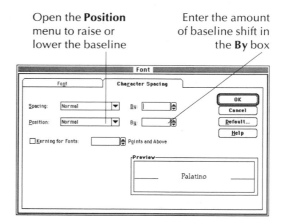

Figure 8 *Character Spacing tab on the Font dialog box controls the baseline of characters.*

Lumps and Bumps Children's Playground

Figure 9 *Logo created by shifting baseline up and down.*

Shifting the Baseline

Choose **Kerning for Fonts** to turn on automatic kerning

Then enter the point size above which you want text kerned

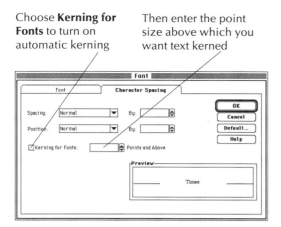

Figure 10 *Kerning for Fonts check box controls automatic kerning.*

Controlling Character Kerning

Kerning is the act of reducing the space between two characters in a font that appear to be spaced too far apart—a common problem, especially in larger sizes of fonts. For example, the characters V I need to be kerned slightly to reduce the unsightly space between the letters. To automatically kern characters:

1 Choose the Font command on the Format menu. Or, to kern only a few characters, highlight the characters first, and then choose the Font command.

2 Choose the Character Spacing tab **(Figure 10)**.

3 Click the **Kerning for Fonts** check box to add an **X**. Then enter the size, above which you want to kern. For example, if you only want to kern the 18 point headlines in a newsletter, but not the 12 point text, enter 18 in the **Points and Above** box.

Tip

◼ Generally speaking, you will not have to kern characters in text sizes. If you do kern text, you will often make the words more difficult to read. Save kerning for larger type sizes **(Figure 11)** which really shout for kerning.

Too much space   Better spacing

Figure 11 *Kerning would close up excess letter space, and improve readability.*

Kerning Type

Adding Special Characters

To add trademarks and copyright symbols, em and en dashes, or curly quotation marks to your documents:

1 Position the insertion point where you want to add the special character.

2 Choose the Symbol command on the Insert menu **(Figure 12)** to display the Special Characters tab of the Symbol dialog box **(Figure 13)**.

3 Click the character you want from the menu. Choose OK to add it to your document.

Tips

◼ If you will be adding more than one character, you needn't close and reopen the Symbol dialog box. Instead, click its title bar and slide it to the bottom of the document window. Then click your document to make it active. Whenever you need to add another character, simply click the top of the dialog box to make it active.

◼ If you use a special character often, such as the registered trademark symbol, note its keyboard shortcut in the menu and use it instead of the dialog box. You could also create a unique keyboard shortcut for the character. In the Special Characters tab, choose the character you want, then click the **Shortcut** button. Press the keyboard combination you want and choose OK to save the shortcut.

Figure 12 *Symbol command on the Insert menu.*

Click the character from the menu, or note the keyboard shortcut and use it after closing the dialog box

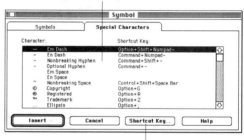

Click to add or change a keyboard shortcut

Figure 13 *Add special characters with the Special Characters tab on the Symbol dialog box.*

Special Characters

Figure 14 *Symbol command on the Insert menu.*

Then click on the dingbat or symbol you want; double-click to add it to your document at the insertion point

Choose the **Font** containing the dingbat you want to use

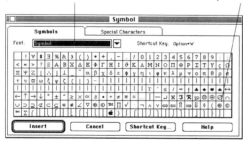

Figure 15 *Symbols tab on the Symbol dialog box shows font dingbats and symbols.*

Adding Dingbats

Dingbats can be any character other than letters, numbers and punctuation marks, including flourishes, bullets, and any number of custom graphics and icons. To add a dingbat:

1 Position the insertion point where you want to add the dingbat.

2 Choose the Symbol command on the Insert menu **(Figure 14)**.

3 Choose the Symbols tab on the Symbol dialog box **(Figure 15)**.

4 Now choose the font for the dingbat symbol you want in the **Font** pop-up menu. As you change fonts in the menu, the respective symbols will change in the list below.

5 Finally, choose the actual symbol, by clicking to highlight and choosing the **Insert** button, or double-clicking the symbol. If you want to add several symbols, you can leave the Symbol dialog box active and move back to your document by clicking anywhere in the document window outside the dialog box.

Dingbats and Symbols

Creating Drop Caps

1 Choose the Drop Caps command on the Format menu **(Figure 16)** to open the Drop Caps dialog box **(Figure 17)**.

2 Select either the more usual drop cap format, which intrudes into the paragraph text, or a hanging drop cap which is outdented into the left margin.

3 Select the font for the drop cap character. Consider selecting a sans serif drop cap if the text is in a serif typeface, or vice versa.

4 Decide how many lines down you want the drop.

5 Finally, enter the amount of standoff between the cap and text in the **Distance from Text** box.

Sample drop caps are shown in **Figure 18**.

Tip

▪ You can also create a drop cap by adding a large initial character in a frame. First, insert the frame at the beginning of the paragraph. In the Frame Format dialog box, choose text wrapping. It's also wise to anchor the frame to the paragraph.

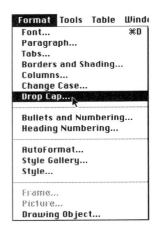

Figure 16 *Drop Cap command on the Format menu.*

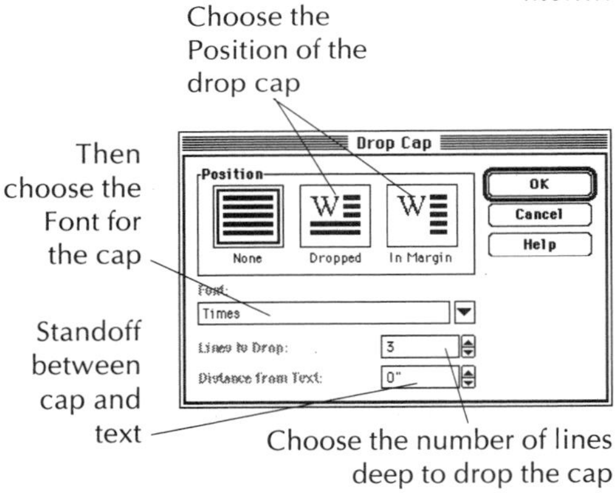

Figure 17 *Define drop caps with the Drop Cap dialog box.*

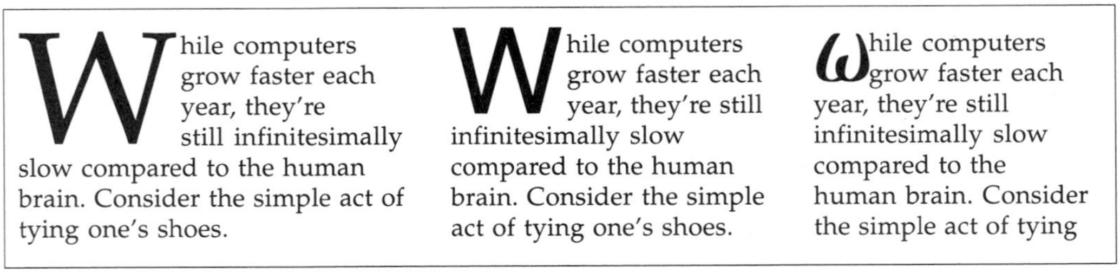

W hile computers grow faster each year, they're still infinitesimally slow compared to the human brain. Consider the simple act of tying one's shoes.

W hile computers grow faster each year, they're still infinitesimally slow compared to the human brain. Consider the simple act of tying one's shoes.

W hile computers grow faster each year, they're still infinitesimally slow compared to the human brain. Consider the simple act of tying

Figure 18 *Different typefaces for the drop cap offer varying looks (left to right are Palatino, Helvetica, and Biffo).*

Figure 19 *Hyphenation command on the Tools menu.*

Click to turn on
automatic hyphenation

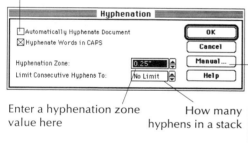

Enter a hyphenation zone
value here

How many
hyphens in a stack

Click for Manual hyphenation

Figure 20 *Tailor hyphenation to your needs with the Hyphenation dialog box.*

Hyphenating Words

One of the easiest ways to dress up your documents is to properly hyphenate words along the right margin. This will even out the right edges of the text (if the text is left-aligned) or even out word spacing (if the text is justified). Word uses a hyphenation dictionary to know where to break words between lines, and allows you to override its decisions with manual hyphenation.

1 Choose the Hyphenation command on the Tools menu **(Figure 19)** to open the Hyphenation dialog box **(Figure 20)**.

2 To start automatic hyphenation click the **Automatically Hyphenate Document** check box to add an **X**.

3 Enter the amount of hyphenation zone—any word that falls into the zone will be considered for hyphenation. The narrower the zone, the more words will be hyphenated.

4 Decide how many consecutive hyphens you want. Unlimited means Word could theoretically end every line with a hyphenated word. Two or more consecutive lines ending with a hyphenated word—known as a *stack* of hyphens—is sometimes considered bad typographical form.

5 To make hyphenation choices yourself, choose the **Manual** button. As Word finds each potential word to hyphenate, it will stop and let you decide what to do with it.

Controlling Hyphenation

Creating Special Type Effects

Special effects include running text around a curve, added graduated fills or special colors, or creating text in interesting shapes.

1 Choose the Object command on the Insert menu **(Figure 21)** to open the Insert object dialog box. Choose **WordArt 2.0** as the Object to open.

2 In the WordArt dialog box **(Figure 22)** type the text you want to modify and choose a shape from the Choose a **Shape** menu **(Figure 23)**.

3 The text you entered will be modified based on the shape you select, and displayed in the Preview box **(Figure 24)**.

4 Choose OK to add the modified text to your document.

Figure 21 *Object command on the Insert menu.*

Type the text you want to modify here

Choose a shape from the shape menu —

Choose the typeface and its characteristics here —

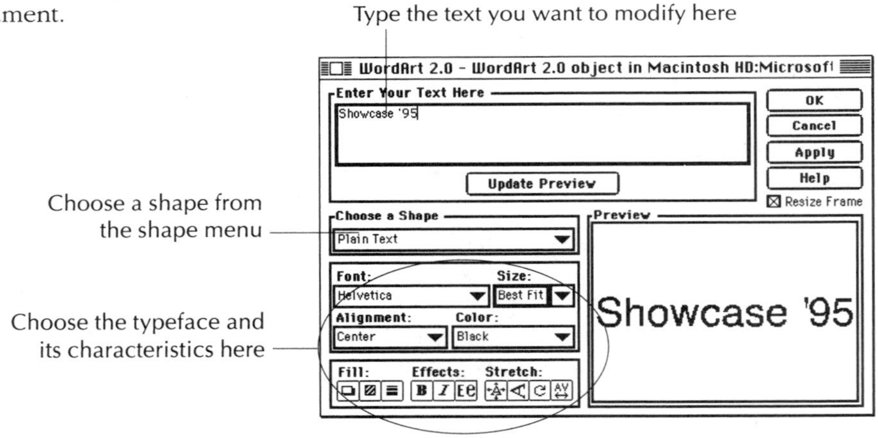

Figure 22 *Add artistic flare to your text with the WordArt dialog box.*

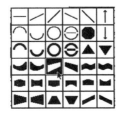

Figure 23 *WordArt shape menu lets you shape text.*

Figure 24 *WordArt Preview box shows what your selection will look like.*

Type Special Effects

File Management

*T*HIS chapter covers the small, but nagging problems we all have with computers: "Now where did I put that file?" "What did I name that last marketing letter?" Why can't I seem to find last month's sales forecast?" "Where did I file the annual report?" As you gain confidence with Word, and your hard disk fills up with letters, reports, invoices, proposals, manuscripts, graphics, clip art, and the like, document management will become increasingly important. While Word doesn't have a full-blown file manager, it sports a nifty search window, shows you the latest files that you've opened, and tracks important document statistics in its document summary window.

Introduction

Opening Recent Files

The easiest way to find files you have worked on recently is to ask Word to display their file names. Here's how:

1 Choose the Options command on the Tools menu **(Figure 1)** to open the Options dialog box.

2 Click the General tab **(Figure 2)**.

3 Now click the **Recently Used Files List** check box to add an **X**. In the **Entries** box enter the number of file names you want Word to track, up to nine.

4 Choose OK to return to your document.

Once you have created or opened one or more documents, their file names will be displayed on the File menu **(Figure 3)**. To open any of the displayed documents, simply click the file name.

Figure 1 *Options command on the Tools menu.*

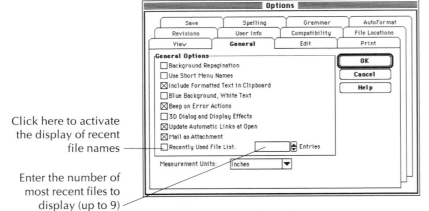

Click here to activate the display of recent file names ——

Enter the number of most recent files to display (up to 9) ——

Figure 2 *General tab on the Options menu controls the display of recently opened file names on the File menu.*

Figure 3 *File menu now displays recently opened files.*

Opening Recent Files

Figure 4 *Summary Info command on the File menu.*

Document Summaries

The information in document summaries helps Word find and keep track of your documents. While filling out the summary dialog box might take a few moments, you'll be glad you did when it comes time to search for that important document.

1 Choose the Summary Info command on the File menu **(figure 4)** to see the Summary Info dialog box **(Figure 5)**.

2 Fill in the boxes for the document's title, subject, key words and any general comments you have. You can add up to 255 characters to any of the fields. Notice that Word fills in your name (or at least, the name listed as user in the User Info tab of the Options dialog box).

3 Click the **Statistics** button to see a summary of your document **(Figure 6)**.

Tips

▪ Word really doesn't care what you add to the Summary Info text boxes, so if your work is project oriented, you might add the name of the associated project in the **Title** text box.

▪ If you work with a number of departments or clients, you might use the **Author** text box to track that information. Then Word can sort your files based on the client or department.

Word will automatically add the first few words of your document as the **Title**

Figure 5 *Information you add to the Summary Info dialog box helps Word search for the document later.*

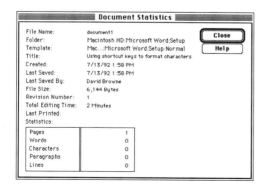

Figure 6 *Statistics dialog box.*

Summaries

About Word's Search Capabilities

Choose the Find File command on the File menu **(Figure 7)** or choose the Find button on the Open dialog box **(Figure 8)**. You will see the Search dialog box **(Figure 9)** the first time you use the Find command. Word lets you define searches, and saves them for you. Once a search has been saved, choosing the Find File command will take you directly to the Find dialog box, described below.

Searching for Files

Word's search features let you define specific search criteria, and save the definition so you can run the search any time. This can be useful, for example, if you needed to see correspondence to certain customers, or review monthly sales activity reports, or look at past overdue invoices—each task could be set up in Word as a specific search. Here's how:

1 Choose the Find File command on the File menu to see the Search dialog box. If you see the Find File dialog box, press the Search button at the bottom.

2 To search for a specific file, type the name in the **File Name** text box. To narrow the search to only one drive or folder, enter the drive and folder names in the location text box.

3 If you want to save the search criteria, choose the **Save Search As** button to open the Save Search As dialog box **(Figure 10),** and enter a description for search criteria.

4 To delete a saved criteria, click the **Delete Search** button.

Figure 7 *Find Files command on the File menu.*

If you can't find the file you want to open, click **Find File** to open the Find Files dialog box

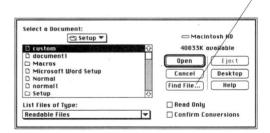

Figure 8 *Click the Find Files button on the Open dialog box to see Word's file search capabilities.*

Searching for Files

Save individual searches by clicking the **Save Search As** button

Once saved, you can choose the search you want in the Saved Searches pop-up menu

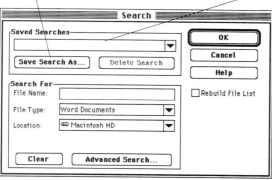

Figure 9 *Use the Search dialog box to set up search criteria for the files you want to find.*

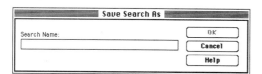

Figure 10 *You can save each set of search criteria as a different search with the Save Search As dialog box.*

Searching for Files

About Advanced Searches

To add to the criteria for a search and further define and narrow the results of the search, choose the Advanced Search button to open the Advanced Search dialog box **(Figure 11)**. The dialog box lets you define the parameters of the search on three tabs:

- ■ **Location**—This tab further limits the boundaries of the search by specifying which folders on the drive you selected in the Search dialog box.

- ■ **Summary**—Remember when I said earlier in this chapter that Word uses the information you enter in the Summary Info dialog box for searches? Here's where you can define the exact criteria for searching summary information.

- ■ **Timestamp**—Here you can specify ranges of dates and times for your search criteria. You might want to only search for files you created this month, for example, or for only last year's financial reports.

Advanced Location Searches

1 From the Search dialog box, choose the **Advanced Search** button to open the Advanced Search dialog box. Then click the Location tab.

2 Next, fill in the different locations on your hard disk to search: click the **Add** button to add the search to the **Search In** box **(Figure 12)**.

3 Click one of the other tabs to add search criteria, or choose OK to return to the Search dialog box.

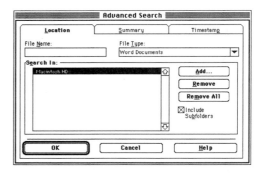

Figure 11 *Location tab on the Advanced Search dialog box searches for files by location.*

Figure 12 *Search In menu shows the current folders Word will look in when searching for your files.*

Advanced Searches

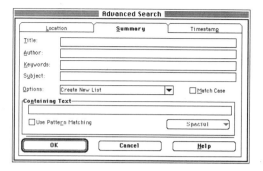

Figure 13 *Summary tab on the Advanced Search dialog box searches for files with summary information.*

Advanced Summary Searches

1 From the Search dialog box, choose the **Advanced Search** button to open the Advanced Search dialog box. Then click the Summary tab **(Figure 13)**.

2 Enter information in the four summary fields (**Title**, **Author**, **Keywords** and **Subject**) that will help Word locate the document you want. If you're unsure of the spelling, use a special search character (see the special search character table below).

3 If you know a phrase or sentence in the document, you can enter it in the **Containing Text** box.

4 Click one of the other tabs to add search criteria, or choose OK to return to the Search dialog box.

Advanced Searches

Special Search Characters	How to Use
?	Replaces any single character (*Cind?* finds *Cindy* and *Cindi*)
*	Replaces any number of characters in sequence (*Ste*en* finds both *Stephen* and *Steven*)
" "	Finds the phrase enclosed inside quotation marks (*"burdened 1994 overhead"*)
\	Tells Word that one of the special characters is used as a normal character
,	Logical OR (*Personnel, Quality* finds files with references to either)
& (or space)	Logical AND (*Personnel & Quality* finds files with both references)
` (tilde)	Logical NOT (`*Personnel* excludes references to Personnel from the search)

Advanced Timestamp Searches

1 From the Search dialog box, choose the Advanced Search button to open the Advanced Search dialog box. Then click the Timestamp tab **(Figure 14)**.

2 Enter a range of dates (in the **From** and **To** boxes) that the document you're searching for was either last saved or created. Keep in mind that the wider the range, the more documents Word will find. If you have more than one person using your computer, or if you are tied to a network, you can enter the name of the person who last saved or created the document in the **By** boxes.

3 Click one of the other tabs to add search criteria, or choose OK to return to the Search dialog box.

About Locating Your Files

Once the search criteria is defined, it's a simple matter to activate the search—by clicking the OK button in the Search dialog box. The results of the search will be displayed in the Find File dialog box **(Figure 15)**. Click the **View** pop-up menu to see one of three views of the search results:

- **Preview**—Lets you see the first page of documents, or a rendering of graphics.

- **File Info**—Shows you information about the file, such as the title and author.

- **Summary**—Indicates the summary and statistical information on the file.

Move the highlight bar to the file you want and choose **Open** to open the file.

Enter a range of **Saved** or **Created** dates for the file you want

Enter the author's name (from the Summary Info dialog box)

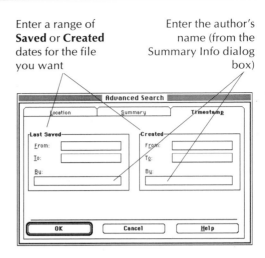

Figure 14 *Timestamp tab on the Advanced Search dialog box searches for files based on their date of creation.*

Figure 15 *Search results are shown in the Find File dialog box.*

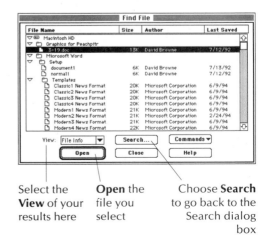

Select the **View** of your results here

Open the file you select

Choose **Search** to go back to the Search dialog box

Figure 16 *Preview view of files listed in the Find File dialog box.*

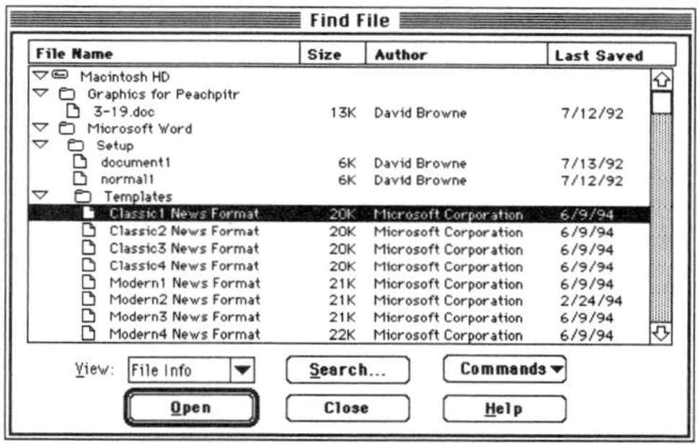

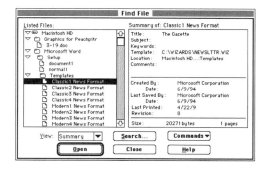

Figure 17 *File Info view of files listed in the Find File dialog box.*

Viewing File Contents

The Find File dialog box can display the contents of just about any file it locates, including Word documents, Word clip art, many other graphic formats, and foreign word processing files. To see the file contents, choose the View menu and select Preview **(Figure 16)**.

Tip

▪ Word can take a long time trying to display some types of large graphic files, such as TIFFs. If you become impatient waiting, just choose Cancel. Word will stop processing the file and display a grayed preview screen.

Viewing File Information

The Find File dialog box can display two different pages of information: file information showing the author, document title (if applicable) and date last saved; and the same summary information Word displays in the Summary Info dialog box.

1 To see file information choose **File Info** from the View menu **(Figure 17)**.

2 To see summary information, choose **Summary** from the View menu **(Figure 18)**.

Figure 18 *Summary Info view of files listed in the Find File dialog box.*

Saving Files

You save your document whenever you choose the Save command on the File menu **(Figure 19)**. The first time you save, Word will ask you for a file name and location; after that saving is a mere blip of your hard disk in the background. To save even faster press **Cmd+S**.

Tip

■ If you have more than one document open, a quick way to save all the documents simultaneously is to choose the Save All command on the File menu. If any documents are new and have not yet been saved, Word will ask you to assign a file name and location.

Figure 19 *Save command on the File menu.*

Click to create automatic backup copies of your work

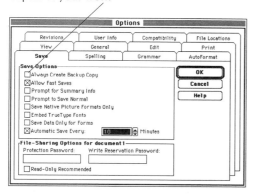

Figure 20 *Save tab on the Options dialog box controls automatic backups.*

Double-click **AutoSave Files** to change the location

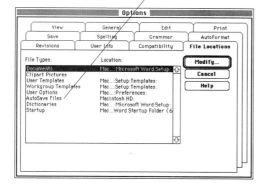

Figure 21 *File Locations tab on the Options dialog box controls where backup copies are automatically stored.*

Creating Backup Copies

If allowed, Word will automatically create a backup copy of each of your files. Just activate the feature, and tell Word where you want the backup stored.

1 Choose the Options command on the Tools menu **(Figure 20)** to open the Options dialog box.

2 Now, click the Save tab **(Figure 21)**.

3 Click the **Always Create Backup Copy** check box to add an X.

4 Now, let's tell Word where we want the backup copies stored. Choose the File Locations tab **(Figure 22)**.

5 Double-click the **AutoSave Files** location and you'll see the Modify Location dialog box **(Figure 23)**. Enter the location to store backup files in the **Location of AutoSaved Files** text box. Choose OK to go back to the Locations tab. Choose OK again to return to your document.

Choose a new AutoSave location here

Click **New** to create a new folder in your hard drive

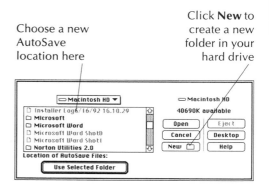

Figure 22 *Enter a new folder for backup files in the Modify Location dialog box.*

Saving One Document as Another

There are a number of reasons you might want to save an existing file as a separate, differently-named file. You may want to use an existing document as the basis for another, similar document. Or, you may want to make a copy of the document on a floppy disk to carry to another computer. Or, you might protect your original document by creating a second document to experiment with. Here are the steps:

1 Choose the Save As command on the File menu **(Figure 24)** to open the Save As dialog box **(Figure 25)**.

2 Enter the name of the file in the **File Name** text box. You can use the same name as the file now has, but a different location to create two copies of the same file (useful when you want to make a copy onto a floppy disk).

3 Choose OK to create the new file.

If you don't change the location and leave the name the same, Word will warn you that you are about to overwrite the existing file. Choose OK to do so, or Cancel to leave the original file intact.

Save the new file in a different format by opening the **Save File as Type** menu and choosing the format

Figure 23 *Save As command on the File menu.*

Type the new name for the document here

Choose a location for the new file here

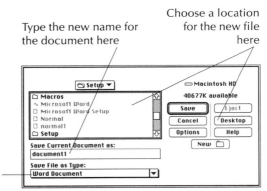

Figure 25 *Save your document with a different name with the Save As dialog box.*

Word Time Savers

*C*ONSIDERING how easy and intuitive Word is to use, you might skip over this chapter on time savers: Don't. These features are really just the tip of the iceberg, but they will get you started in the right direction. Wizards are found in almost all Microsoft products—they are a quick and simple way to learn how to design documents while the actual design work is done for you. Macros are one of the easiest ways of speeding up monotonous word processing chores. Word's sorting capabilities are quick to use (often requiring only that you choose the command and click OK in the dialog box). Bookmarks and annotations help you create and revise large volumes. Word's AutoText and AutoCorrect commands offer a unique approach to saving you time and effort.

Once you grow comfortable with these simple aids, take a look at Word's powerful macro language which allows you to build complete, customized applications. Check out the full power of Word's sorting capabilities. And use Word's automatic text and correction commands to save hours of typing and proofing when you work with larger documents.

Introduction

About Wizards

Wizards do the design work; you fill in the pertinent details when the Wizard asks. Word comes with a number of Wizards that handle the creation of everything from business letters to award certificates; from fax cover pages to calendars; and from meeting notices to dunning notices. Once the Wizard is through designing your document, you are free to change anything you want—the document is no different than if you had created it from scratch.

Using Wizards

1 Choose the New command on the File menu **(Figure 1)** to display the New dialog box **(Figure 2)**. Wizards are grouped among templates in the **Template** pop-up menu.

2 Choose the Wizard you want from the list. For this example, let's choose the Memo Wizard.

3 In a moment you will see the first Memo Wizard dialog box **(Figure 3)**. To walk through the design steps and answer any questions the Wizard may have, choose the **Next** button. (To bypass the steps and questions, and complete the memo as quickly as possible, choose **Finish**.)

Figure 1 *New command on the File menu.*

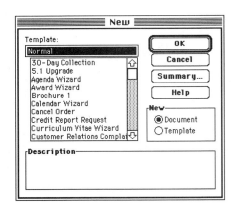

Figure 2 *New dialog box includes Word's Wizards.*

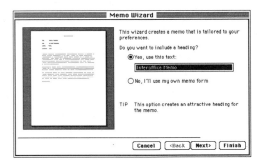

Figure 3 *Memo Wizard's opening dialog box begins a memo layout.*

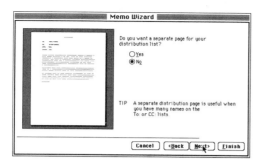

Figure 4 *Memo Wizard's second dialog box specifies how to handle the distribution list.*

4 The second Memo Wizard dialog box asks you about the distribution list **(Figure 4)**. Press **Next** to continue.

5 The Wizard now has questions on the basic layout of the menu **(Figure 5)**.

6 The next dialog box concerns how the bottom of the memo—writer's and typist's initials, enclosures, and so forth—will be handled **(Figure 6)**.

7 Next, you will tell the Wizard how you want the memo's header and footer **(Figure 7)**.

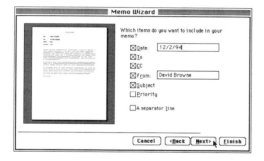

Figure 5 *Memo Wizard's third dialog box continues customizing the memo.*

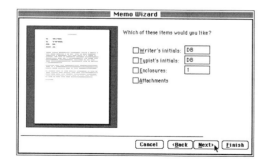

Figure 6 *Memo Wizard's fourth dialog box covers the bottom of the memo.*

Figure 7 *Memo Wizard's fifth dialog box handles page headers and footers.*

Using Wizards

8   The next to the last dialog box is common to all Wizards: it determines which font to use **(Figure 8)**. **Classic** is set in a serif typeface, **Contemporary** is set in a sans serif face and **Typewriter** is set in Courier.

9   The final dialog box, also common to all Wizards, asks if you would like to display interactive help after the design is completed **(Figure 9)**. Choose **Finish** to complete the design **(Figure 10)**.

Now, simply add the pertinent details, shown in brackets, and your memo is ready to print.

Figure 8 *Memo Wizard's sixth dialog box specifies the style of typography.*

Figure 9 *Memo Wizard's final dialog box.*

Date:	05/24/94
To:	[Names]
CC:	[Names]
From:	David Browne
Subject:	[Subject]
Priority:	[Urgent]

[Type your memo text here]

DB/DB

Enc. 1

Attachments

Figure 10
Finished memo created by a Word Wizard.

Using Wizards

Figure 11 *Macro command on the Tools menu.*

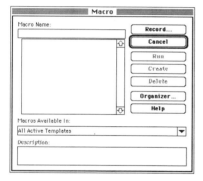

Figure 12 *Record and play back macros with the Macro dialog box.*

Stop recording button

Resume recording button

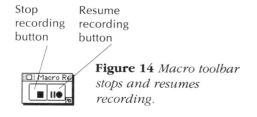

Figure 14 *Macro toolbar stops and resumes recording.*

Recording Macros

A macro is a series of steps that is recorded and played back, much like an audio tape is used. For example, you can record the steps to create an index entry (see Chapter 15) as a macro. Then, instead of going through the individual steps, you can simply run the macro—less steps that take less of your valuable time.

1 Choose the Macro command on the Tools menu **(Figure 11)** to open the Macro dialog box **(Figure 12)**.

2 Choose the **Record** button. Word will display the Record Macro dialog box **(Figure 13)**.

3 Enter a name for the macro in the **File Name** text box and choose OK. The dialog box will close, the mouse arrow will change to a macro recording icon, like this: 🔲 And you will see the Macro toolbar **(Figure 14)**.

4 The macro is now recording everything you do. Carry out whatever steps you want included in the macro. When you're done, click the Stop button on the Macro toolbar.

Type the new macro name

Choose where to assign the macro

Choose the template for this macro

Write a description of the macro's functions

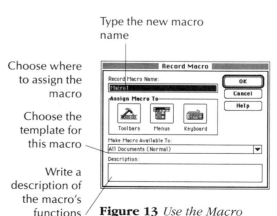

Figure 13 *Use the Macro Record dialog box to prepare new macros.*

Playing Macros

1 Choose the Macro command on the Tools menu **(Figure 15)** to open the Macro dialog box **(Figure 16)**.

2 Select the macro you want to play from the list, and choose the **Run** button.

Tip

▧ A faster way to run a macro is to add it as a command to one of the pull-down menus, or as a button on a toolbar (see Appendix A for help in customizing Word to your needs).

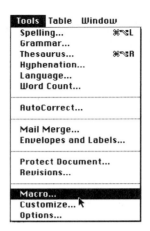

Figure 15 *Macro command on the Tools menu.*

Click **Run** to play the macro

Enter the macro name

Or, choose a macro from the list

Descriptions help explain the function of each macro

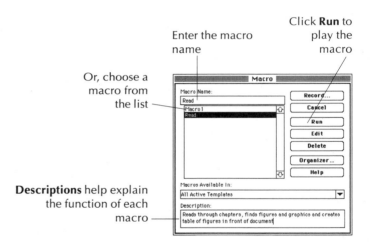

Figure 16 *Choose the macro you want to play with the Macro dialog box.*

```
Zack
Judy
Bob
Sam
Elliot
David
Abe
```

Figure 17 *List of names ready to be sorted alphabetically.*

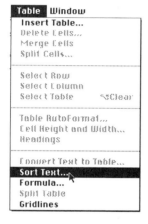

Figure 18 *Sort Text command on the Table menu.*

About Sorting Items

The sort command renumbers lists, rearranges the order of paragraphs, and sorts information in tables. It is just waiting to help save you time, without you having to do a thing except activate the command.

Alphabetizing Lists

1 Create a list of words you want to alphabetize **(Figure 17)**. Highlight the names you want to sort.

2 Choose the Sort Text command on the Table menu **(Figure 18)**. You will see the Sort dialog box open **(Figure 19)**. Notice that the dialog box is already set to alphabetize the names.

3 Click OK to begin sorting. Word will rearrange the names in alphabetic order from A to Z **(Figure 20)**.

Sorting defaults to alphabetizing lists (preset to sort **Paragraphs** of **Text**)

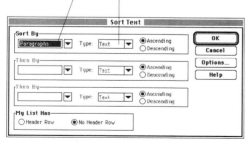

Figure 19 *When text is selected, Sort dialog box defaults to alphabetic sorts.*

```
Abe
Bob
David
Elliot
Judy
Sam
Zack
```

Figure 20 *List of names rearranged in alphabetic order.*

Sorting Lists

Sorting Numbers in Order

1 Create a column of numbers **(Figure 21)** and highlight those numbers you want Word to put in order.

2 Choose the Sort command on the Table menu to open the Sort dialog box **(Figure 22)**. Notice here that Word has changed the Type box from *Text* to *Number.* Again, you need only click OK to sort the numbers in ascending order **(Figure 23)**.

14647.08
11743.31
14541.89
13657.00
10191.19
16230.70

Figure 21 *Column of numbers ready to be sorted in ascending order.*

Sorting defaults to ascending numbers (preset to sort **Paragraphs** of **Numbers**)

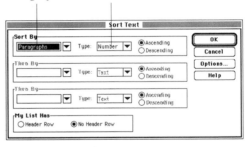

Figure 22 *When a column of numbers is selected, Sort dialog box defaults to ascending-order sorts.*

Figure 23 *Column of numbers rearranged in ascending order.*

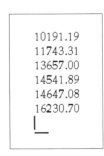

10191.19
11743.31
13657.00
14541.89
14647.08
16230.70

This is the first paragraph of text which I would really like to be second. If it were in second position I'd be much happier, but I'm too lazy to drag and drop it along with rearranging the other paragraphs.
This is the second paragraph, which I'd rather have as the first paragraph. Using the Sort command, I can easily move its position from second to first.
This is the third paragraph, which I will leave alone. It is a nice little paragraph all by itself.

Figure 24 *Paragraphs needing rearrangement.*

2This is the first paragraph of text which I would really like to be second. If it were in second position I'd be much happier, but I'm too lazy to drag and drop it along with rearranging the other paragraphs.

1This is the second paragraph, which I'd rather have as the first paragraph. Using the Sort command, I can easily move its position from second to first.

3This is the third paragraph, which I will leave alone. It is a nice little paragraph all by itself.

Figure 25 *Add a number, in the order you want the paragraphs, as the first character in each paragraph.*

1This is the second paragraph, which I'd rather have as the first paragraph. Using the Sort command, I can easily move its position from second to first.
2This is the first paragraph of text which I would really like to be second. If it were in second position I'd be much happier, but I'm too lazy to drag and drop it along with rearranging the other paragraphs.
3This is the third paragraph, which I will leave alone. It is a nice little paragraph all by itself.

Figure 26 *Word sorts the paragraphs by number, thus rearranging them in the order you want.*

Sorting Paragraphs

Word can just as easily change the order of paragraphs as it can single words. By adding a number as the first character in each paragraph, you can control how Word reorganizes the paragraphs.

1 Type three paragraphs of text **(Figure 24)**.

2 To rearrange the order of the paragraphs, add the numbers 1,2,3 to the paragraphs in the order you would like them rearranged **(Figure 25)**.

3 Highlight the paragraphs you want rearranged, and choose the Sort command on the Table menu.

4 In the Sort dialog box, choose **Number** as the type to sort by. Then click OK to start the sort. Word will rearrange the numbers in ascending order, and rearrange the paragraphs at the same time **(Figure 26)**.

Sorting Paragraphs

Creating Bookmarks

Bookmarks take you to specific areas of your document. Bookmarks can mark the location of graphics, frames, tables, or embedding or linked objects. You can have as many bookmarks as you want.

1 Select the text you want to mark as a bookmark.

2 Choose the Bookmark command on the Edit menu **(Figure 27)** to open the Bookmark dialog box **(Figure 28)**.

3 Type the name for the selection in the **Bookmark Name** box. The name you add can have up to 40 characters, but no spaces (use the underline or hyphen character to substitute for the space).

4 Choose **Add** to add the name to the Bookmark list.

5 Choose OK to return to your document.

Figure 27 *Bookmark command on the Edit menu.*

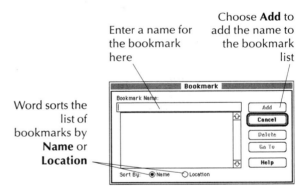

Enter a name for the bookmark here

Choose **Add** to add the name to the bookmark list

Word sorts the list of bookmarks by **Name** or **Location**

Figure 28 *Store and find bookmarks with the Bookmark dialog box.*

Bookmarks

Double-click here or here to open the Go To
dialog box

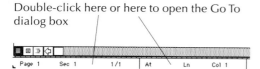

Figure 29 *Clicking the status bar opens
the Go To dialog box.*

Choose **Bookmark**
from the list

Enter the page number,
if known, for the
bookmark you want

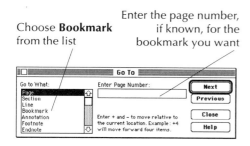

Figure 30 *Go To dialog box can take you
to any bookmark.*

Finding Bookmarks

Once you've created a bookmark, it's a
simple matter to find it:

1 Double-click the Page/Section box or
the Position box on the status bar
(Figure 29).

2 You will see the Go To dialog box open
(Figure 30).

3 Choose **Bookmark** from the Go to
What menu.

4 Then, click the **Enter Bookmark
Name** to find the bookmark you want.
Click the **Go To** button to move to the
bookmark.

Tip

■ The Go To dialog box is one of those
dialog boxes that can stay displayed
while you work in your document. To
keep it active, yet out of the way, click
the title bar and drag it down, until all
but the title bar is off the screen, in front
of Word's status bar **(Figure 31)**.

Word's status bar   Go To dialog box

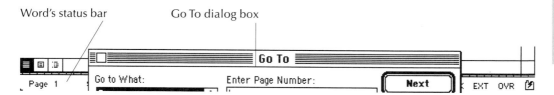

Figure 31 *Go To dialog box can remain active as you work in your document (here it is
slid down over the bottom status bar, ready for use).*

Creating Annotations

Annotations let you add comments to your document, without affecting the document itself. Annotations are most often used to add review comments to documents—each reviewer's annotation is numbered with their initials. But, annotations can just as easily be notes or reminders to yourself, or last minute details you must remember.

1 To add an annotation, position the insertion point where you want the annotation marker to appear. If your annotated comment refers to a selection of text, highlight the text.

2 Choose the Annotation command on the Insert menu **(Figure 32)** to open the Annotation pane **(Figure 33)**.

3 Notice that your initials are added automatically to the beginning of the annotation. Now type the text of the annotation.

4 Choose **Close** to return to your document.

Tips

▪ The annotation pane can remain visible while you continue to work in your document. Click the black bar at the top edge of the pane and drag it up to increase its size, or down to reduce its size.

▪ A quick way to display the Annotation pane is to press **Cmd+Option+A**.

Figure 32 *Annotation command on the Insert menu.*

Word adds the reviewer's initials and the annotation number

Click the **From** menu to select the reviewer for the annotation

Click to add sound annotations

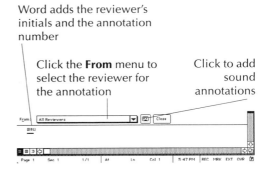

Figure 33 *Annotation window pane.*

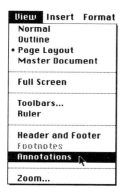

Figure 34 *Annotations command on the View menu.*

[DB1]This·sections·needs·more·support·evidence,·check·with·the·technical·lib
[DB2]The·paragraphs·in·section·3A·should·be·moved·closer·to·the·beginning.
[DB3]Do·we·really·want·to·state·our·pricing·this·early???¶
[DB4]This·resume·should·be·the·model·for·all·the·others;·very·impressive!¶
[DB5]Wasn't·it·Bennett·that·we·did·the·followon·work·for?·Let's·mention·it·as
[DB6]Double·check·the·spelling·of·the·last·names·here.¶

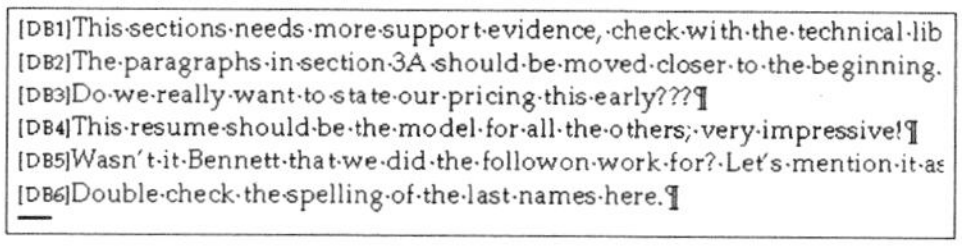

Figure 35 *Annotation examples in the Annotation pane.*

Figure 36 *Print command on the File menu.*

Figure 37 *Choose Annotations in the Print menu to print annotations and page number references.*

Viewing Annotations

1 Choose the Annotations command on the View menu **(Figure 34)** to open the Annotation pane **(Figure 35)**.

2 The annotations you have made are visible in the window pane. To move the insertion point in the document to a specific annotation, click the annotation you want in the pane.

Tip

◼ If you work in long documents containing lots of headings or figures, use the annotation feature to help you move around in the documents. For each heading, create an annotation with the heading name (or figure numbers if you are working with lots of figures). Keep the annotation pane open while you work. To move forward or backward through your document to a specific heading, simply click the annotation in the pane—the insertion point will jump to that annotation in the document.

Printing Annotations

1 Choose the Print command on the File menu **(Figure 36)** to open the Print dialog box **(Figure 37)**.

2 Click the **Print What** pop-up menu and choose Annotations.

3 Click OK to print a listing of all annotations and their page numbers.

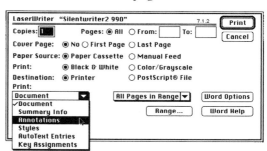

Annotations

Creating AutoText

Word's AutoText feature (called *glossaries* in Word 5) adds text or graphics automatically with the click of a custom button. AutoText is useful any time you need to repeatedly add the same phrase, or the same graphic. For instance, you might create an AutoText entry to add a standard closing to your business letters, or a graphic to your company letterhead. To create an AutoText entry:

1 Highlight the text or select the graphic you want to add as an AutoText entry.

2 Choose the AutoText command on the Edit menu **(Figure 38)** to open the AutoText dialog box **(Figure 39)**.

3 Enter a name for this entry in the **Name** text box. The entry itself is displayed in the Preview box.

4 Click the **Add** button to add the entry to the AutoText list.

Figure 38 *AutoText command on the Edit menu.*

Give the AutoText entry a name here

Click **Insert** to add the entry to the list

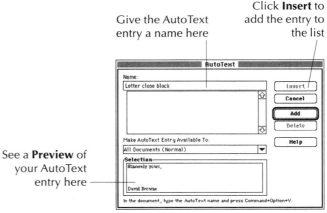

See a **Preview** of your AutoText entry here

Figure 39 *Save repeated text or graphics in the AutoText dialog box.*

Figure 40 *AutoText command on the Edit menu.*

Using AutoText

1 Position the insertion point where you want to add the text or graphic AutoText entry.

2 Choose the AutoText command on the Edit menu **(Figure 40)** to open the AutoText dialog box **(Figure 41)**.

3 Click the entry you want to add, and choose the **Insert** button.

Tip

◼ You can save the formatting of text you add as an AutoText entry by including the paragraph marker when you select the text. To display the markers, click the hide/reveal paragraph symbol button on the Standard toolbar.

Click the AutoText entry you want to add to your document

Click **Insert** to add the text or graphic

AutoText

| Name: |
| Letter close block |

Letter close block

Insert
Cancel
Add
Delete
Help

Insert As
● Formatted Text   ○ Plain Text

Preview
Sincerely yours,

David Browne

In the document, type the AutoText name and press Command+Option+V.

Figure 41 *Add saved text or graphic AutoText entries to your documents with the AutoText dialog box.*

AutoText

Using AutoCorrect

AutoCorrect is an ingenious feature that can correct typos, substitute words for abbreviations, and insert words or phrases based on a code you select.

1 Choose the AutoCorrect command on the Tools menu **(Figure 42)** to open the AutoCorrect dialog box **(Figure 43)**.

2 Use the **Replace** box to add the word, abbreviation or code you will type.

3 Use the **With** box to add what you want AutoCorrect to replace the word, abbreviation, or code with.

4 Click **Add** to add the text to the AutoCorrect list. To change an existing entry, scroll down the list, and click the entry you want. The entry will be added to the Replace and With boxes. Make any needed changes and click Add again.

Now, whenever you type the phrase you entered in the Replace box, Word will automatically substitute the phrase you added to the With box.

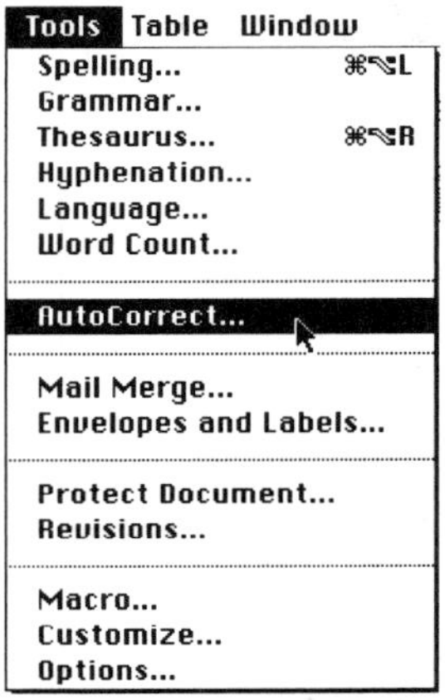

Figure 42
AutoCorrect command on the Tools menu.

Enter the word to you want "corrected" And its replacement

Choose the automatic options you want

Then, click **Add**

Shows you the currently defined AutoCorrect entries

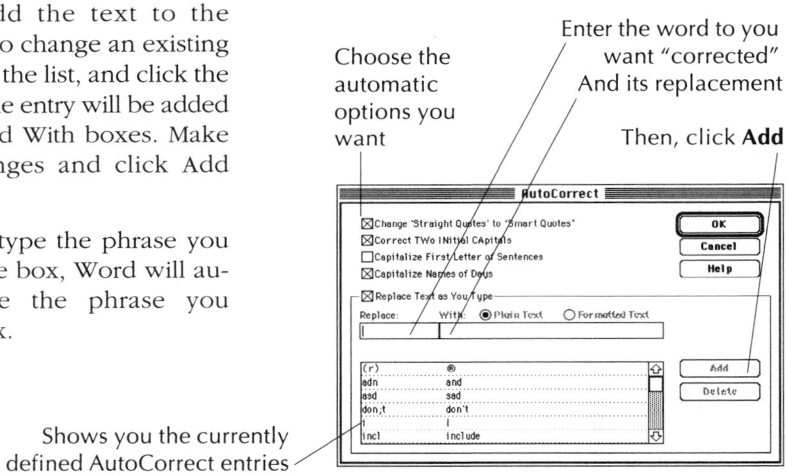

Figure 43 *AutoCorrect dialog box.*

Examples of AutoCorrect Entries

Replace	With
het hte eht	*the*
msword	*Microsoft Word 6 for Macintosh*
co	*The Industrial Tool, Die and Design Company, Inc.*
arci	*architectural renderings to scale*
mac	*Macintosh PowerBook Duo 230*
con	*United States House of Representatives*
~d	*David Browne & Associates*

AutoCorrecting Your Work

Styles

*T*HINK about the moment-by-moment things you do to format a document: there are the normal tasks of setting a typeface, or font, for body copy, and different fonts for different levels of headlines or headings. Then there are the steps to establish patterns of sizes for the headings (the more important the heading is, the larger and/or bolder its size should be). Then comes finer, detailed work like setting up tab and indent settings, line spacing, column measurements, and the like. Finally, there's the really nit-picky stuff, like specifying frames, formatting bullets for bulletted lists, or adding a lined or shaded border to paragraphs.

Taken individually, the tasks of designing and formatting a single-page document seem easy; however, multiply the tasks by dozens, if not hundreds of pages and all the individual steps can take enormous time and concentration. So use *styles* instead.

Styles are collections of formatting decisions that are assigned to paragraphs of text. One style may have all the formatting for body text (and be labeled as such), another for first level headings, and still another for text in tables. You can have as many styles as you like. The real advantage of a style is when it comes time to alter formatting. Instead of going through your document to make individual changes, you simply change the style, and all the paragraphs assigned to the style are automatically changed.

Defining New Styles

1 Choose the Style command on the Formatting menu **(Figure 1)** to open the
Style dialog box **(Figure 2)**.

2 Click the **New** button to open the New
Style dialog box **(Figure 3)**.

3 Name the style. Then, choose whether
the style is applied to characters or paragraphs. Decide if another style normally
follows the assignment of this new style
(a body text style would normally follow a heading style, for instance).

4 You can base the style on any existing
style, or start from scratch.

5 Now, click the **Format** button **(Figure
4)** and choose which areas of the style
you want to define. For each choice on
the menu, you can move to that respective formatting dialog box to specify
some aspect of formatting for the style.

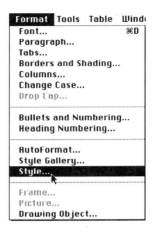

Figure 1 *Style command on
the Format menu.*

List shows the
current styles
in use

Paragraph and character
previews of the current style

New creates a new style

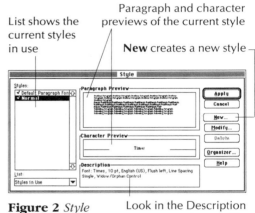

Figure 2 *Style
dialog box.*

Look in the Description
area for specific
elements of the style

Name the style

Choose a **Character** or
Paragraph style

You can base the
attributes of this
style on any
other

Which style (if any)
should follow this
style

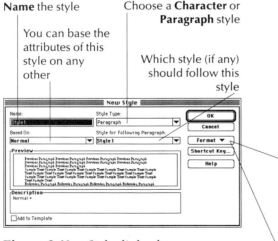

Figure 3 *New Style dialog box.*

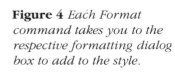

Figure 4 *Each Format
command takes you to the
respective formatting dialog
box to add to the style.*

Defining Styles

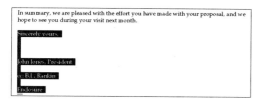

Figure 5 *To apply a style, first highlight the text to be affected.*

Figure 6 *Choose a style from the Standard toolbar.*

Using Existing Styles

Word comes with a wide variety of styles already defined, including styles for brochures, technical manuals, tables of contents, tables of authorities, business letters and much more. To assign text with any of these styles:

1 Click the insertion point in the paragraph you want to assign a style to, or highlight the text that will receive the style **(Figure 5)**.

2 From the Standard toolbar, **Shift+Click** the pop-up **Style** menu to see all of Word's styles **(Figure 6)**.

3 Choose the style. In the case of our example, click the signature style, and the text containing the insertion point will take out all the attributes of the style **(Figure 7)**.

Figure 7 *The highlighted text will assume the attributes of the style (in this case indenting the letter signature block).*

Using Styles

Displaying Style Names

Word displays the current style assigned to your work on the Standard toolbar **(Figure 8)**. Click open the menu to see all styles assigned to the current template **(Figure 9)**. (To see all styles, **Shift+click** the menu to open it.) Sometimes it's helpful to see styles for more than one paragraph at a time. To display style names in the left margin:

1 Choose the Options command on the Tools menu **(Figure 10)** to open the Options dialog box.

2 Click the View tab **(Figure 11)**.

3 In the Window area of the dialog box, click the **Style Area Width** box and increase its width from 0 to .5 inches or more.

4 Click OK to return to your document. You will now see the style names displayed in the left margin.

Current style in use

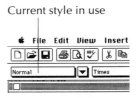

Figure 8 *Standard toolbar shows currently selected style.*

Figure 9 *Style menu shows current styles available.*

Style Area means the left page margin: set a width of at least .5 inches to see styles

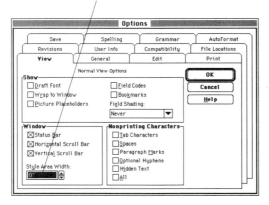

Figure 11 *Specify style names in the left margin with the Options dialog box.*

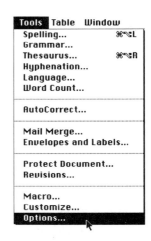

Figure 10 *Options command on the Tools menu.*

Displaying Style Names

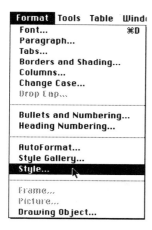

Figure 12
Style command on the Format menu.

Changing the Default Style

When you click the new document button on the standard menu and begin typing, Word applies the default Normal style to your words. You can make any changes you like to the default style.

1 With the style selected, choose the Style command on the Format menu **(Figure 12)**. You will see the Style dialog box **(Figure 13)**.

2 Notice that the style you're currently using is displayed. Click the Modify button to change the current style (in this case the Normal style).

3 In the Modify Style dialog box **(Figure 14)**, open the Format menu, and make whatever changes you want.

4 When you close the Styles dialog box, the changes you made will take effect.

Tips

■ A quick way to modify the default style's formatting is to highlight text already containing the formatting you want, open the Font dialog box (on the Format menu) and click the Default button. Word will apply all formatting from the selected text to the default style.

■ You can use the Style dialog box to modify any style, or create new styles. Simply select the style you want to change, open the Modify dialog box, and make the changes.

Current style's paragraph and character previews

Click **Modify** to change the style

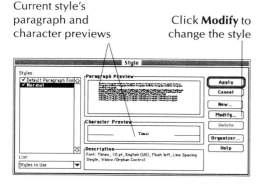

Figure 13 *Style dialog box shows attributes for the current style.*

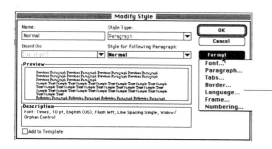

Click any **Format** menu command to open a format dialog box and modify the existing style attributes

Figure 14 *Change attributes of the current style with the Modify Style dialog box.*

Using the Style Gallery

Once the text of your document is roughed out, it's easy to apply a special style to it using the Style gallery.

1 Choose the Style Gallery command on the Format menu **(Figure 15)** to open the Style Gallery dialog box **(Figure 16)**.

2 Choose the template that contains the styles you want to apply to your document.

3 If you click the **Document** radio button in the Preview area, Word will apply the styles to your words. Click the **Example** button to see a finished example of the template styles. Finally, click the **Style Sample** button to see samples of the actual styles.

4 Click OK to apply the template styles you choose to your document.

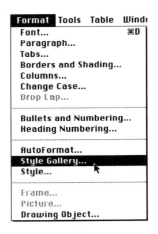

Figure 15 *Style Gallery command on the Format menu.*

Click the **Template** you want in the list

Click **Example Preview** to see a pre-designed example of what the styles in the template look like

Preview can also apply the styles to your **Document**, or display actual **Style Samples**

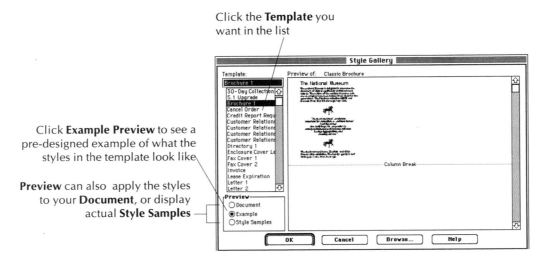

Figure 16 *Style Gallery dialog box manages and previews Word's templates and styles.*

Click the **Organizer** button to move to the Organizer dialog box

Figure 17 *Style dialog box.*

Copying Styles

Word uses a clever dialog box called the *Organizer* to copy styles from one document to another.

1 Choose the Style command on the Format menu to open the Style dialog box **(Figure 17)**.

2 Choose the **Organizer** button to open the Organizer dialog box **(Figure 18)**.

3 Find the file in the left-hand list box that contains styles you want to copy. In the right-hand list, find the file you want to copy the styles to.

4 Click the **Copy** button to perform the copying. Use the **Close File** buttons to close the current files and locate new files **(Figure 19)**.

In the left-hand list, choose the styles in the document you want to add to a template

Click **Copy** to copy the style into the template

Click **Close File** to choose the document you want

Click **Close File** to choose the template you want

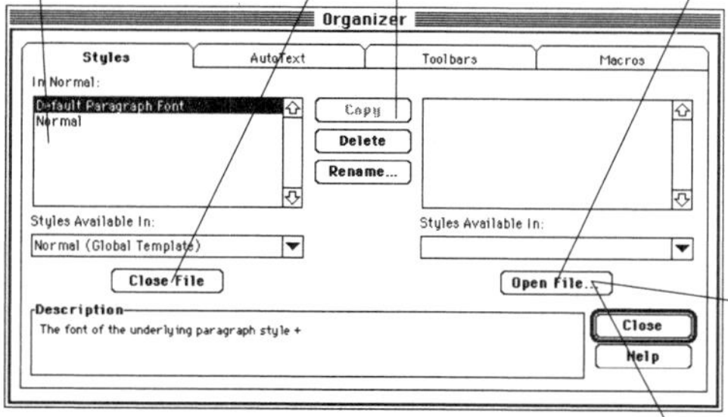

Figure 18 *Organizer dialog box adds styles you want to use to templates.*

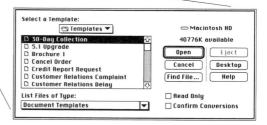

Figure 19 *Use the Open dialog box to locate either the document or the template.*

Style Keyboard Shortcuts

Assigning a style you like to a keyboard shortcut means you can activate the style by simply pressing a key combination.

1 Choose the Style command on the Format menu to open the Style dialog box **(Figure 20)**.

2 Click the **Modify** button to move to the Modify dialog box **(Figure 21)**.

3 Click the **Shortcut Key** button to open the Keyboard tab on the Customize dialog box **(Figure 22)**.

4 Click the **Categories** box to find Styles. Then choose the style you want in the **Commands** box. Finally, press a combination of the Command key, Option key and a third letter or number key to create the shortcut.

Choose the style you want for a keyboard shortcut

Click the **Modify** button to move to the Modify dialog box

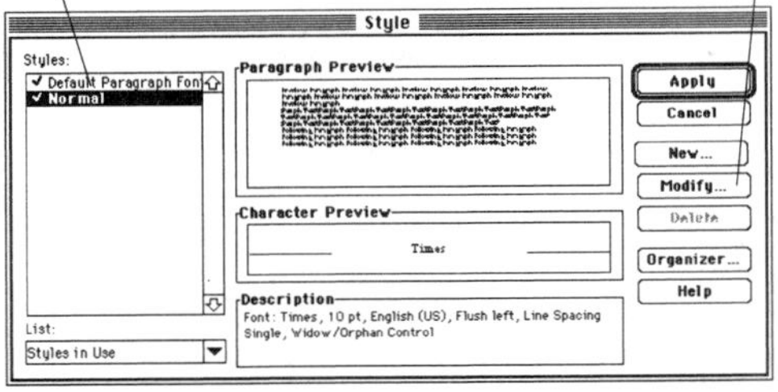

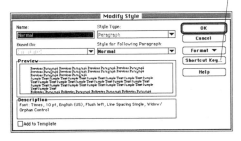

Figure 20 *Style dialog box.*

Click the **Shortcut Key** button to move to the Customize dialog box

Figure 21 *Modify Styles dialog box.*

Hold down the Command and Option keys and press a third key to record the keyboard shortcut (it will be shown here)

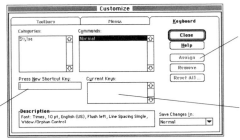

Click the **Assign** button to record the key combination

Currently assigned key combinations are shown here

Figure 22 *Define keyboard shortcuts with the Keyboard tab on the Customize dialog box.*

Style Keyboard Shortcuts

Tables

*T*ABLES are a way to organize information in tabular form rather than lines of text. Tables consist of columns and rows of information--columns are vertical groups of information (or *cells*) that go across the page; rows are a stack of horizontal cells that go down the page. While you can create the look of columns and rows by setting tab stops across the page, sometimes it's much simpler to create a table than to fool around with a bunch of tab positions.

The best means of introducing you to the concept of tables is to think about a restaurant menu. Menus have columns across the page, containing entrees, descriptions and prices; and rows down the page of menu items. To find what you want in a menu, you look down the rows to the item you like, and across the columns to read the description and find the price. Any table works the same way: the combination of columns and rows helps you locate what you need to know quickly and efficiently.

If you need to create an instant table in Word, the easiest way is to click the Insert Tables button on the Standard toolbar **(Figure 1)**, drag the point diagonally across and down to select the number of columns and rows **(Figure 2)** and release the mouse button. Your table will be added automatically at the insertion point position.

Introduction

Figure 1 *Tables button on the Standard toolbar gives you instant tables.*

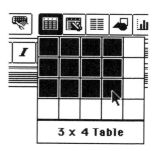

Figure 2 *Click the tables button and drag out the number of rows and columns you need to create a table.*

Using the Table Wizard

If your tabular needs run to a more complex table, the table Wizard will design, lay out and build the table to your specifications.

1 Choose the Insert Table command on the Table menu **(Figure 3)** to open the Table dialog box **(Figure 4)**.

2 Click the **Wizard** button to start the table Wizard. The Wizard steps are shown in Figures 5 through 12.

3 After the Wizard finishes work, it leaves you in the Table AutoFormat dialog box **(Figure 13)** to add the finishing touches.

4 Choose from the list of table styles to dress up your table. Click OK to add the table to your page at the insertion point position **(Figure 14)**.

Figure 3 *Insert Table command on the Table menu.*

Click **Wizard** to let Word design a table for you

Figure 4 *Insert Table dialog box.*

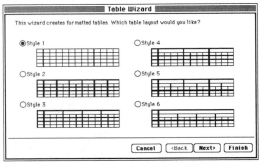

Figure 5 *Initial Table Wizard dialog box.*

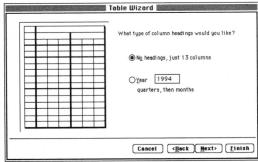

Figure 6 *Wizard asks about column headings.*

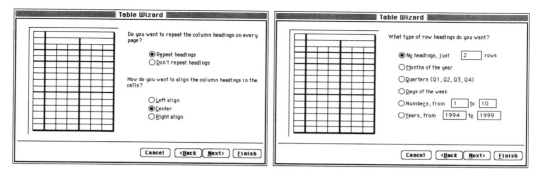

Figure 7 *Wizard sets column headings.*   **Figure 8** *Wizard sets row headings.*

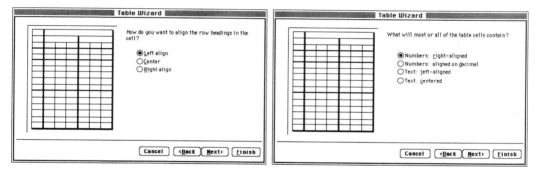

Figure 9 *Wizard sets alignment within cells.*

Figure 10 *More questions about cell alignment.*

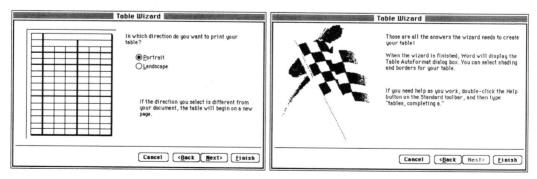

Figure 11 *Wizard sets page orientation.*

Figure 12 *Final Wizard dialog box asks if you want interactive help as you work.*

Table Wizard

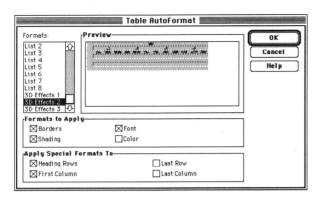

Figure 13 *Final Wizard dialog box takes you to AutoFormat to finish your table design.*

	1995											
	Q1			Q2			Q3			Q4		
	Jan	Feb	Mar	Apr	May	Jun	Jul	Aug	Sep	Oct	Nov	Dec
Jan												
Feb												
Mar												
Apr												
May												
Jun												
Jul												
Aug												
Sep												
Oct												
Nov												
Dec												

Figure 14 *Finished table, compliments of the Table Wizard, ready for you to fill in data.*

Figure 15 *Insert Table command on the Table menu.*

Creating Tables

1 Position the insertion point where you want a table to be added.

2 Choose the Insert Table command on the Table menu **(Figure 15)** to open the Insert Table dialog box **(Figure 16)**.

3 Enter the number of columns and number of rows you want. Leave the Column Width set to Auto. For now, just choose OK to add the table (we'll cover AutoFormat in a moment).

Select the number of columns and rows here

Choose
Column Width
to specify the
width of
columns (**Auto**
sets columns of
equal width)

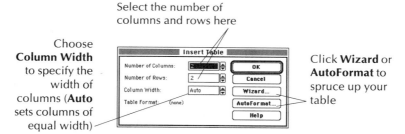

Click **Wizard** or
AutoFormat to
spruce up your
table

Figure 16 *Create simple tables with the Insert Table dialog box.*

Adjusting Row Height

1 Click the insertion point in the cell you want to resize (highlight all rows if you want to adjust the height of all cells in the table.

2 Choose the Cell Height and Width command on the Table menu **(Figure 17)**.

3 You will see the Row tab on the Cell Height and Width dialog box **(Figure 18)**.

4 Open the **Height of Rows** menu. Choose Auto to let Word accommodate the tallest entry in a cell. Select **At Least** to set a minimum height and let Word adjust if needed to accommodated a taller entry. Choose **Exactly** to specify the exact height of the row of cells.

5 Choose the **Previous Row** or **Next Row** buttons to adjust the previous or next row.

Figure 17 *Cell Height and Width command on the Table menu.*

Choose **Auto** to let Word adjust height

Choose the **Alignment** of text within cells here

Move to the **Previous** or **Next** row, and specify the row height

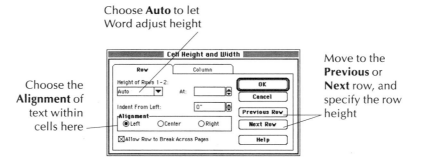

Figure 18 *Cell Height and Width dialog box adjusts the size of rows and columns in tables.*

Adjusting Row Sizes

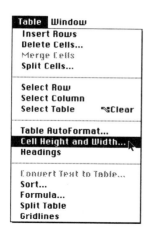

Figure 19 *Cell Height and Width command on the Table menu.*

Choose a Space Between Columns value to specify the gutter between columns

Select the width for the table column

Or choose **AutoFit** to let Word adjust the column width

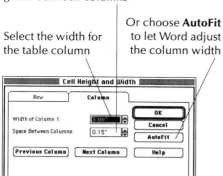

Figure 20 *Adjust the width of columns with the Columns tab on the Cell Height and Width dialog box.*

Adjusting Column Width

1 Click the insertion point in the cell you want to resize (highlight all rows if you want to adjust the width of all cells in the table.

2 Choose the Cell Height and Width command on the Table menu **(Figure 19)** to open the Cell Height and Width dialog box. Click the Column tab **(Figure 20)**.

3 Enter the width of the column in the **Width of Column** text box.

4 To change the margin (or *gutter*) between columns, enter a value in the **Space Between Columns** text box.

5 Alternately, you can click the **AutoFit** button and have Word resize the column for you.

6 To resize the previous or next column, click the appropriate button.

Tip

■ You can quickly adjust the position of columns in you table by positioning the insertion point over the column guide you want to move. The insertion point will change to an adjustment pointer **(Figure 21)**. Click and drag the vertical guide that separates the columns to the right or left.

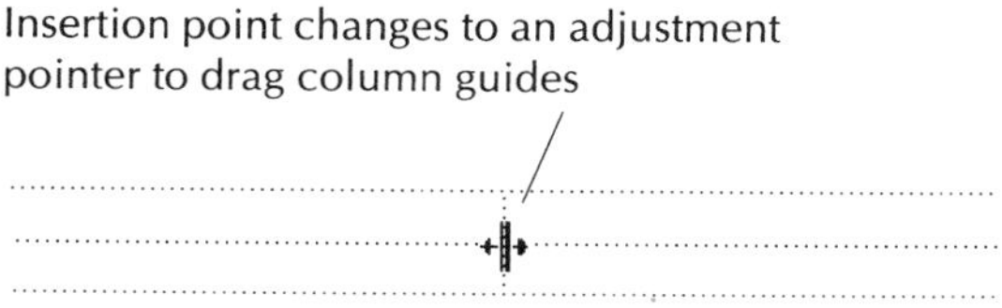

Insertion point changes to an adjustment pointer to drag column guides

Figure 21 *Adjust column width the mouse by clicking and dragging a column guide.*

Adjusting Column Sizes

AutoFormatting Tables

The table formatter offers 33 different styles to dress up the columns and rows of your tables.

1 Click the insertion point anywhere inside the table.

2 Choose the Table AutoFormat command on the Table menu **(Figure 22)** to open the Table AutoFormat dialog box **(Figure 23)**.

3 Choose the table style from the Formats list; you'll see a rendering of the format in the Preview box.

4 Select the areas of formatting you want applied to your table, by clicking the check boxes you want in the Formats to Apply area. You can experiment with the formatting further, by clicking the options in the Apply Special Formats To area.

5 Choose OK to apply the formatting to your table.

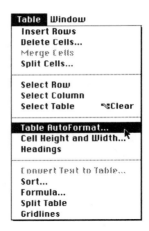

Figure 22 *Table AutoFormat command on the Table menu.*

Pick a **Format** from the list (the **Preview** box displays the style of each format you click)

Click the applicable check boxes to apply the format you selected to your table

Click these check boxes to apply special formatting to your table

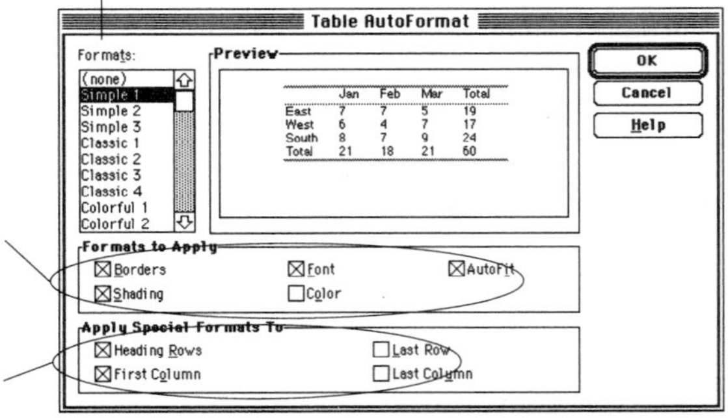

Figure 23 *Create a professional-looking table instantly with the Table AutoFormat dialog box.*

Moving Between Cells

1 Press the **Tab** key to move forward and down through each cell in your table. To move backward, hold down the **Shift** key and press **Tab**.

2 To move down by row, press the **Down Arrow** key. Press the **Up Arrow** key to move up by rows.

3 To move immediately to the first cell in a row, hold down the **Option** key and press **Home**. Hold down the **Option** key and press **End** to move to the last cell in a row.

4 Press **Option+Page Up** to move to the top cell in a column, or **Option+Page Down** to move to the bottom cell in a column.

Where to Move	What to Press
Forward to the next cell	Tab
Backward to the previous cell	Shift+Tab
Down to next row	Down Arrow
Up to previous row	Up Arrow
First cell in row	Option+Home
Last cell in row	Option+End
Top of column	Option+Page Up
Bottom of column	Option+Page Down

Moving Around in Tables

Adding Graphics

1 Click the insertion point in the cell you want to add a graphic in.

2 Choose the Picture command on the Insert menu **(Figure 24)** to open the Insert Picture dialog box **(Figure 25)**.

3 Find the graphic you want to add to your table and choose OK to add the graphic **(Figure 26)**.

Once a graphic is added, it's easy to dress up your table to a professional level. Just read the next two pages on customizing tables.

Figure 24 *Picture command on the Insert menu.*

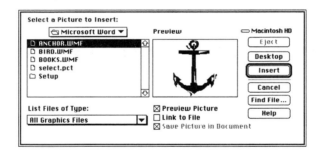

Figure 25 *Insert Picture dialog box.*

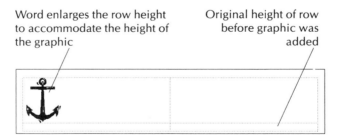

Word enlarges the row height to accommodate the height of the graphic

Original height of row before graphic was added

Figure 26 *When a graphic is added to a table cell, Word adjusts the height and width of the cell to accommodate the size of the graphic.*

Graphics in Tables

Customizing a Table

Click and drag the column guide to the left to widen the right column for a title

Figure 27 *Left column width is adjusted using the mouse.*

Once a graphic is added to a plain Jane table, let's see how easy it is to dress up the rows and columns. First, we'll move the column guide to make room for a title.

1 Position the insertion point over the column guide and it will change to an adjustment tool **(Figure 27)**. Click the guide and drag to the left so the anchor graphic is nicely boxed **(Figure 28)**.

2 Now add a title by clicking in the first row of the wide column and typing the title **(Figure 29)**.

For this table we actually need three columns: one to list the week of charters, one to list the type of boat, and the third to list the respective charter price. In order to keep the title running across the columns, we'll have to split the wider column into two narrower columns.

3 Click the insertion point in the wider column, in the second (lower) row.

Column guide moved to the left

Figure 28 *Left column now boxes the graphic; wider right column allows for a title.*

Figure 29 *Table title added to right-hand column.*

Customizing Tables

4 Choose the Split Cells command from the Table menu **(Figure 30)** to open the Split Cells dialog box **(Figure 31)**.

5 Since you want to split the cell into two columns, choose the number 2 in the Number of Columns text box, and choose OK. The cell will be split into two cells (which will become columns in just a minute when we add more rows **(Figure 32)**.

6 Add rows to your table by clicking the insertion point in the bottom row, and choosing the Insert Rows command on the Table menu **(Figure 33)**. Word will automatically add one row to the bottom of your table. Now add several more rows.

7 Finally, choose a table format from the Table AutoFormat dialog box, add some column headings and results can be very attractive **(Figure 34)**.

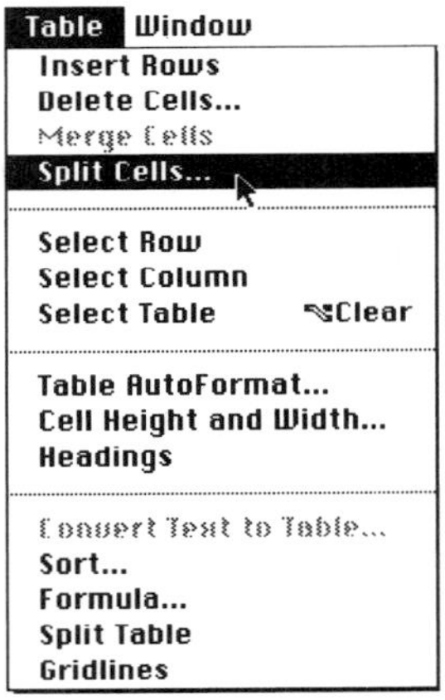

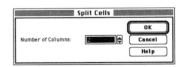

Figure 30
Split Cells command on the Table menu.

Figure 31 *Split Cells dialog box.*

Right-hand column split into two columns

Figure 32 *Split the column in the row below the title to get the number of columns you need.*

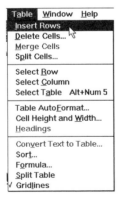

Figure 33 *Add the number of rows you need with the Insert Rows command on the Table menu.*

Figure 34 *Finished table complements of AutoFormat.*

Customizing Tables

Figure 35 *Caption command on the Insert menu.*

Adding Table Captions

You may want to add captions to tables in more formal documents. Words makes adding captions a breeze:

1 Position the insertion point just above or below the table, where you want the caption placed.

2 Choose the Caption command on the Insert menu **(Figure 35)** to open the Caption dialog box **(Figure 36)**.

3 Click the **Label** menu to choose Table as the label. Word will automatically number the caption, shown in the Caption text box.

4 Click in the **Caption** box to add the title for this table (if you want tables to have titles in your document).

5 Choose the position of your captions with the Positions menu (table captions usually go above tables).

6 Word will number the captions for you. To change the numbering style, click the **Numbering** button.

Caption box shows what caption will be added

Click the **Label** menu to choose **Table**

Then choose the **Position** of the caption

To change the label *Table* to something else (like *Chart, Scenario,* or *Illustration*) click **New Label**

Click to change the **Numbering** style for this caption

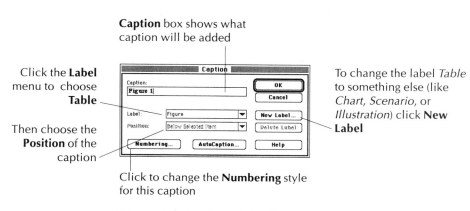

Figure 36 *Caption dialog box defines captions for tables.*

Table Captions

Adding Automatic Table Captions

If you activate automatic captions, Word will add captions to all your tables. Here's how:

1 Choose the Caption command on the Insert menu to open the Caption dialog box **(Figure 37)**.

2 Click the **AutoCaption** button to display the AutoCaption dialog box **(Figure 38)**.

3 Scroll down the list and choose Microsoft Word 6.0 Table **(Figure 39)**.

4 Click the **Label** and **Position** buttons to define the caption, and choose OK to activate automatic captions.

Click **AutoCaption** to open the AutoCaption dialog box

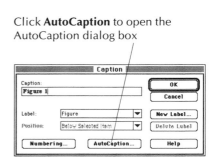

Figure 37 *Caption dialog box.*

Choose the object for which you want to create automatic captions

Determines the type of caption label

Determines caption placement

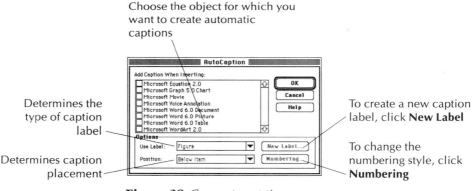

To create a new caption label, click **New Label**

To change the numbering style, click **Numbering**

Figure 38 *Generate captions automatically with the AutoCaption dialog box.*

Figure 39 *Scroll down the object list to find* Word 6.0 Table.

Table Captions

Spelling

A spelling checker sounds like a marvelous feature, especially to those of us who can't spell their way out of a wet paper bag. However, if you think Word will automatically correct *all* your misspelled words, you'll be disappointed. To ensure your words are correct, keep in mind a few ground rules:

- Word accepts what you write with literal meaning—it doesn't know what you *intended* to write, nor the conclusions you *meant* to draw. Word's spelling works only by comparing each of the words in your document to a very large list of words in its dictionary. Any discrepancies are noted—you must tell the software what word you really wanted to use.

- Special vocabularies, for science, medicine (even computers) won't be recognized by Word's spelling program. To handle specialized words, Word lets you create custom dictionaries.

- Take care with alternative spellings (*catalog* and *catalogue*). When the spelling checker displays alternative spellings, be sure you are consistent in choosing the same spelling of the word.

While it's unwise to rely strictly on Word's spelling dictionary, you can employ Word's AutoCorrect feature to catch some of the common typing mistakes many of us make. For example, say you constantly misspell the word *Connecticut*, by adding a second *"t."* It's easy to add the misspelled word (and its correct spelling) to the AutoCorrect dialog box **(Figure 1)**.

Introduction

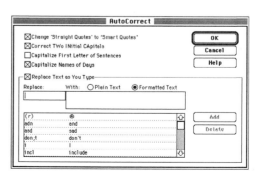

Figure 1 *AutoCorrect dialog box "catches" your typos and corrects automatically.*

Spell-Checking Documents

Spelling is as simple as choosing the command and waiting to see if Word finds any discrepancies. If none are found, Word will close the speller and report that everything is spelling correctly. Here are the steps:

1 Choose the Spelling command on the Tools menu **(Figure 2)** to start Word's spell checker.

2 If Word finds a word not in its dictionary, it will open the Spelling dialog box **(Figure 3)** and display the offending word in the Not in Dictionary text box.

3 If the dialog box shows a suggested word in the Change to box—which is the correctly spelled version of the word you want—click the **Change** button. If the Change to box is empty, click the **Suggest** button to see suggested spellings. Double click the correctly-spelled word in the Suggestions box to change the misspelling. If the dialog box shows a word not in the speller's dictionary which is spelled correctly, click **Ignore** to have the speller ignore this instance of the word.

Figure 2 *Spelling command on the Tools menu.*

The word in question is shown here

This is Word's best guess as to what it should be

Click **Ignore** to skip the word this time, or **Ignore All** to skip the word entirely

Click **Change** to correct the word this time, or **Change All** to correct the word throughout the document

Click **Add** to add the word to the dictionary

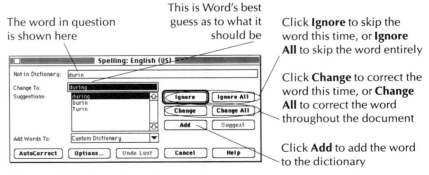

Figure 3 *Spelling dialog box.*

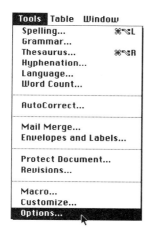

Figure 4 *Options command on the Tools menu.*

Changing Spelling Options

Word offers you several ways to customize the spell-checker to your specific needs.

1 Choose the Options command on the Tools menu **(Figure 4)** to open the Options dialog box **(Figure 5)**.

2 Choose the Spelling tab **(Figure 6)**.

3 Make the changes you want to the way Word checks spelling.

Click **Spelling** to see the Spelling tab

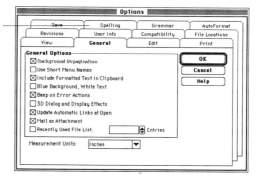

Figure 5 *Options dialog box.*

To spell-check words you told the speller to ignore, click here

Click **Always Suggest** to display possible corrections

Click to see suggestions from only the main dictionary

Choose up to 10 custom dictionaries

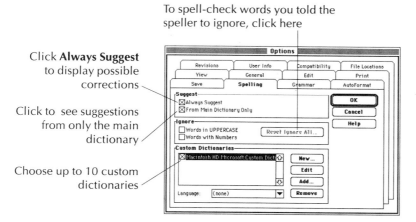

Figure 6 *Spelling tab on the Options dialog box.*

Customizing the Speller

Creating Custom Dictionaries

It is usually a good idea not to add special-ized words that may have different uses or meanings in everyday language to the main spelling dictionary. Instead, acro-nyms, abbreviations and technical jargon should go in custom dictionaries that you create. Here's how:

1 Choose the Options command on the Tools menu to open the Options dia-log box. Now choose the Spelling tab **(Figure 7)**.

2 To create a new custom dictionary, click the **New** button to open the Create Cus-tom Dictionary dialog box **(Figure 8)**.

3 To add a custom dictionary to the list in the dialog box, click **Add** to open the Add Custom Dictionary dialog box **(Figure 9)**.

4 To make a dictionary active, click its check box in the Custom Dictionaries list.

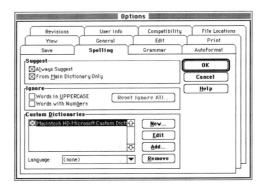

Figure 7 *Spelling tab on the Options dialog box lets you create custom dictionaries.*

Figure 8 *Create Custom Dictionary dialog box saves new dictionaries.*

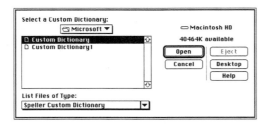

Figure 9 *Add Custom Dictionary dialog box adds dictionaries to the Custom Dictionaries list in the Options dialog box.*

Visio	Aldus
VESA	Asymetrix
IDE	Browne
Browne	EISA
FreeHand	Ethernet
OLE	FreeHand
ISA	gigabytes
Asymetrix	IDE
InfoWorld	InfoWorld
MapInfo	ISA
Micrografx	MapInfo
Netware	Meg
Aldus	Micrografx
Orlando	Netware
PCI	nonscence
EISA	OLE
PhotoStyler	Orlando
PowerMac	PageMaker

Figure 10
Unsorted list for custom dictionary.

Figure 11 *List is sorted with Word's Sort command.*

Converting Documents to Dictionaries

A dictionary is merely a Word document containing a list of words. If you already have a specialized list, you can resave it as a Word dictionary. Here's how:

1 Create a list of words down the page **(Figure 10)**. While it's not necessary, you can alphabetize the list for quicker spelling, by choosing the Sort Text command on the Table menu. Once in the Sort Text dialog box, simply press OK to sort the list of words **(Figure 11)**.

2 Choose the Save As command on the File menu to open the Save As dialog box **(Figure 12)**.

3 Choose a unique name for your dictionary and save it as a dictionary instead of a Word document in the Word Extensions folder.

4 Finally, make the dictionary active by selecting it in the Spelling tab on the Options dialog box.

Tip

■ Here's how to organize words for a quick and easy glossary of terms. First, create a custom dictionary and add all the specialized vocabulary in your document, book or manual as a part of spell-checking the words. Next, save the dictionary as a document. Finally, use the Sort Text command on the Table menu to organize the list in alphabetic order. Add the definitions to the list, and your glossary is complete.

Enter a name for the custom dictionary here

Select **Custom Dictionary** from the Save File as Type menu

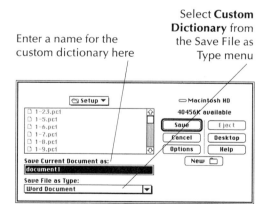

Figure 12 *Use the Save as dialog box to save the word list as a custom dictionary.*

Counting Words

Once your words are spelled correctly, you may want to know how many you wrote. Word has two ways of getting a word count:

1 Choose the Word Count command on the Tools menu **(Figure 13)** to open the Word Count dialog box **(Figure 14)**.

2 Word will immediately count all the words in your document, excluding any words in headers and footers. You can also include in the count all words in footnotes and endnotes by clicking the **Include Footnotes and Endnotes** check box.

You can also count the words in your document as a part of viewing summary information. Here's how:

1 Choose the Summary Info command on the File menu to open the Summary Info dialog box **(Figure 15)**.

2 Choose the Statistics button to see the Statistics dialog box **(Figure 16)**.

3 In the lower half of the dialog box will be the page and words count for your document.

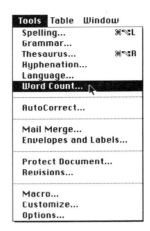

Figure 13 *Word Count command on the Tools menu.*

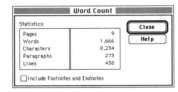

Figure 14 *Word Count dialog box.*

Figure 15 *Summary Info dialog box.*

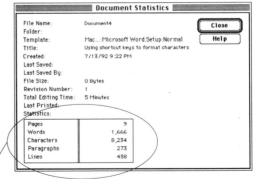

Same results as Word Count dialog box

Figure 16 *Statistics dialog box.*

Counting Words

Find and Replace

*F*_{**IND**} and replace turns your computer loose to do what it does best: search meticulously through your documents, comparing every character to what it's looking for, and changing what you ask it to change. Find and Replace can save you enormous amounts of time and energy. The replace command can also royally screw up your documents if you're not careful how you use it.

Generally speaking, trouble often stems from asking Word to carry out "global" find and replace instructions automatically. Word takes what you ask it to do quite literally; and if you don't carefully consider the literal ramifications of your instructions, they can wreck havoc with your files. Usually you have asked Word to find a part of a word (such as looking for Mac and changing it to Macintosh). You then tell Word to go ahead and change all instances of the word. Word not only changes the name Mac to Macintosh, but creates some new words, like: *Macintoshabre* for *macabre, Macintoshhine* for *machine*, and *Macintoshe* for *mace.* Had you stopped at each instance of the word *Mac,* you could have avoided the mistakes.

Word's Find and Replace commands feature a number of options that let you search for not only words, but also character and paragraph formatting, styles, and virtually any character (or space) in your documents. You can use the Find and Replace commands in conjunction with a macro to perform complex format changes to your documents.

Finding Words

1 Choose the Find command on the Edit menu **(Figure 1)** to open the Find dialog box **(Figure 2)**. An easy shortcut is to press **Cmd+F** to open the dialog box.

2 Enter what you want to find in the Find What text box. If you've run previous searches, you will see those entries by clicking the down arrow button **(Figure 3)**.

3 Click one of the check boxes to restrict your search to certain conditions **(Figure 4)**.

4 Click **Find Next** to find the next occurrence of what you're looking for.

Figure 1 *Find command on the Edit menu.*

Type what you want to search for in the **Find What** text box

Click **Find Next** to locate the next instance of what's in the **Find What** box

Click the **Search** menu to control the direction of the search

Click **Replace** to open the Replace portion of the dialog box

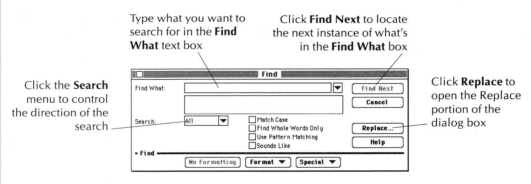

Figure 2 *Find dialog box can look for words, phrases, fonts, formatting, styles and much more.*

Click the check boxes that apply to your search

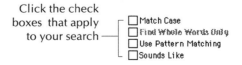

Figure 3 *The Find What text box lists all the search entries you make during a Word session.*

Figure 4 *Check boxes limit your search results to specific criteria.*

Finding Words

Figure 5 *Replace command on the Edit menu.*

Replacing Words

1 There are three ways to open the Replace dialog box:

■ Open the Find dialog box and click the **Replace** button.

■ Use the Replace keyboard shortcut **Cmd+H**.

■ Choose the Replace command on the Edit menu **(Figure 5)** to open the Replace dialog box **(Figure 6)**.

2 Enter what you want to search for in the Find What text box.

3 Enter the replacement word in the Replace With box.

4 Click **Find Next** to move to the first occurrence of the word you're searching for, and click **Replace** to the replace the word.

Enter the replacement text in the **Replace With** text box

Click **Replace** to replace the first instance of the search

Click **Replace All** to replace all instances of the search

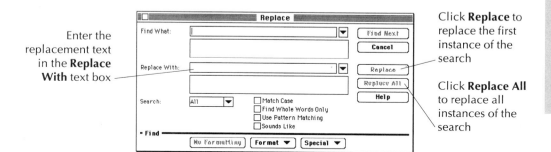

Figure 6 *Replace dialog box adds a replacement section to the Find dialog box.*

Replacing Words

Finding and Replacing Fonts

Using the Find and Replace commands, you can search through your document and substitute any font (or font characteristics) with any other font. Here are the steps:

1 Open the Find dialog box **(Figure 7)**.

2 Leave the Find What text box blank. Click the **Format** button and choose the **Fonts** command.

3 You will see the Find Font dialog box open **(Figure 8)**. Choose the Font and font characteristics you want to search for. *(Continued on next page.)*

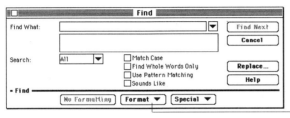

Click the **Format** button and choose **Fonts** to select font characteristics to search for

Figure 7 *To find fonts or font characteristics, click the **Format** button in the Find dialog box, and select **Fonts**.*

Click **OK** to add the characteristics to the Find dialog box

Click the **Font** or **Character Spacing** tab, and specify what you want Word to search for

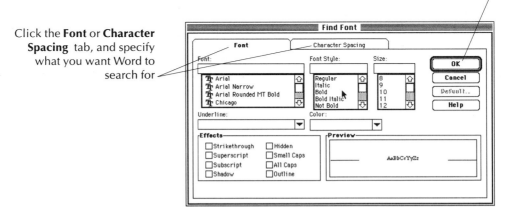

Figure 8 *Specify exactly what characteristics of a font you want to find with the Find Font dialog box.*

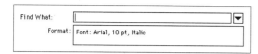

Figure 9 *Font characteristics are added in the Format section of the Find What text box.*

Figure 10 *Clicking the **Replace** button on the Find dialog box changes it to the Replace dialog box.*

4 Click OK to return to the Find dialog box. Notice that the font formatting you specified is detailed in the format box **(Figure 9)**.

5 Now, click the **Replace** button to open the Replace dialog box **(Figure 10)**.

6 Again, leave the Replace With box blank and click the **Format** button.

7 Choose the Font command from the menu to open the Replace Font dialog box **(Figure 11)**.

8 Select the replacement font and its characteristics. Choose OK to return to the Replace dialog box.

9 Finally, click **Find What** to locate the first instance of the font you want to replace, and click **Replace** to substitute the replacement font.

Click **OK** to add the characteristics you select to the Replace dialog box

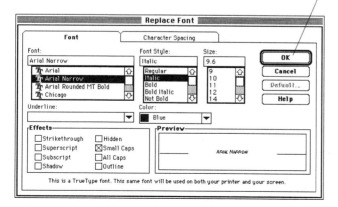

Figure 11 *Use the Replace Font dialog box to specify exactly what font characteristics you wish to replace.*

Finding and Replacing Paragraph Formatting

Word can search and replace specific paragraph characteristics as easily as it replaces font characteristics. Here's how:

1 Open the Find dialog box **(Figure 12)**.

2 Leave the Find What text box blank. Click the **Format** button and choose the Paragraph command.

3 You will see the Paragraph dialog box open **(Figure 13)**. Choose the paragraph formatting characteristics you want to search for.

4 Click OK to return to the Find dialog box. Notice that the paragraph formatting you specified is detailed in the format box **(Figure 14)**. *(Continued on next page.)*

Figure 12 *Search for paragraph formatting by clicking the* **Format** *button and choosing Paragraph from the menu.*

Click **OK** to add the paragraph formatting to the Find dialog box

Specify paragraph formatting on the **Indents and Spacing** and **Text Flow** tabs

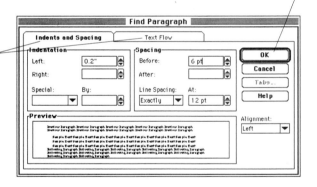

Figure 13 *Use the Find Paragraph dialog box to specify the paragraph formatting you want to search for.*

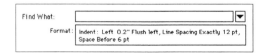

Figure 14 *The Format area of the Find What text box shows the paragraph formatting you specified in the Find Paragraph dialog box (above).*

Paragraph Formatting

The formatting you are searching for

Click **Format** to add the formatting you will substitute here

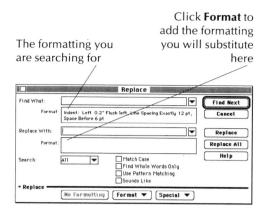

Figure 15 *The Replace dialog box showing the paragraph formatting you want to search for.*

Click the two tabs and choose the paragraph formatting values you want to replace

Click **OK** to add the formatting to the Replace dialog box

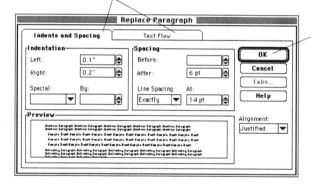

Figure 16 *Use the Replace Paragraph dialog box to select the paragraph formatting you want to replace in your document.*

5 Now, click the **Replace** button to open the Replace dialog box **(Figure 15)**.

6 Again, leave the Replace with box blank and click the **Format** button.

7 Choose the Paragraph command from the menu to open the Paragraph dialog box **(Figure 16)**.

8 Select the replacement paragraph characteristics. Choose OK to return to the Replace dialog box.

9 Finally, click **Find What** to locate the first instance of the paragraph with the characteristics you want to replace, and click **Replace** to substitute the replacement paragraph formatting.

Paragraph Formatting

Finding and Replacing Styles

Styles are another item that Word can search out and change. Here's how:

1 Open the Find dialog box **(Figure 17)**.

2 Leave the Find What text box blank. Click the **Format** button and choose the Style command.

3 You will see the Find Style dialog box open **(Figure 18)**. Choose the style you want to search for.

4 Click OK to return to the Find dialog box. Notice that the style name you selected is shown in the format box **(Figure 19)**. *(Continued on next page.)*

Figure 17 *Find the styles you want to replace by clicking* **Format** *on the Find dialog box.*

Choose the style you want from the **Find What Style** list

Click **OK** to add the style to the Find dialog box

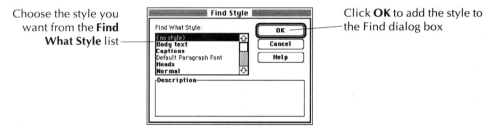

Figure 18 *Use the Find Style dialog box to choose the style you want to locate and replace.*

Figure 19 *The style you choose will be added to the Format area of the Find What text box in the Find dialog box.*

Figure 20 *Click **Format** in the Replace dialog box to select the replacement style.*

5 Now, click the Replace button to open the Replace dialog box **(Figure 20)**.

6 Again, leave the Replace with box blank and click the **Format** button.

7 Choose the Style command from the menu to open the Replace Style dialog box **(Figure 21)**.

8 Select the replacement style, and choose OK to return to the Replace dialog box.

9 Finally, click **Find What** to locate the first instance of the style you want to replace, and click **Replace** to substitute the replacement style.

Choose the style you want as the replacement style from the **Replace With Style** list

Click **OK** to add the style to the Replace dialog box

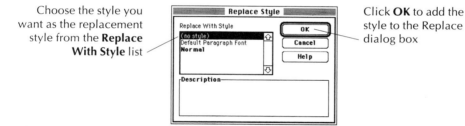

Figure 21 *Select the substitute style in the Replace Style dialog box.*

Changing Double Hard Paragraph Returns to Single Returns

A common problem when importing text from another word processing program is eliminating double carriage returns at the end of paragraphs. While it adds an extra line of space between paragraphs, the double hard returns—which you can see by clicking the Show paragraph symbols button **(Figure 22)**—are not the correct way to add spacing between paragraphs. Here's how to quickly remove them:

1   Open the Find dialog box **(Figure 23)**.

2   Click the **Special** button and choose **Paragraph Mark** from the pop-up menu. Notice that Word adds a ∧ (caret symbol over the number 6 on the keyboard) and the letter **P**. This is Word's code for the paragraph code. (You needn't remember the code; just choose the symbol from the Special menu.)

3   Now choose the Special menu a second time and add a second **∧P** to the Find What box. The two codes tells Word to search only for instances of two consecutive hard return codes. *(Continued on next page.)*

Click **Format** and choose Paragraph Mark twice to find double return codes

Coming·into·the·harbor,·sails·furled·tightly,·the· boat·lost·her·engine.·She·drifted·slowly· broadside·to·the·waves.·The·rockly·inlet·was·no· place·to·loose·steerage,·and·the·wind·picked·up· out·of·the·east,·as·a·sudden·testimony·to·what· was·about·to·happen.¶
¶
From·the·shore·you·could·barely·make·out·the· actions·of·the·skipper·and·mate.·But·on·the·boat,· you·could·almost·feel·that·the·end·was·near.·Her· engine·cranked·until·the·battery·was·dead.·The· keel·touching·the·rocky·bottom·was·a·solid·jar.¶
¶
Now·the·skipper·hurried·to·get·out·an·anchor,· which·seems·to·refuse·to·catch·and·hold.·The· yacht·settled·against·the·rocks·of·the·jetty,·where· she·was·ground·and·crushed·like·so·many·match· sticks.¶
¶

Figure 22 *Word can automatically replace double paragraph returns (shown in the text) with single returns.*

Figure 23 *Use the **Format** button in the Find dialog box to locate paragraph return codes.*

Finding and Fixing Double Returns

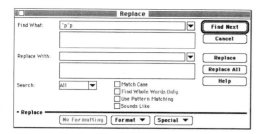

Figure 24 *Replace dialog box with two paragraph codes in the Find What text box.*

```
Paragraph Mark
Tab Character
Caret Character
Clipboard Contents
Column Break
Em Dash
En Dash
Find What Text
Manual Line Break
Manual Page Break
Nonbreaking Hyphen
Nonbreaking Space
Optional Hyphen
Special
```

Figure 25 *The* **Special** *button opens a Codes menu that includes the Paragraph Mark code.*

4 Click the **Replace** button to open the Replace dialog box **(Figure 24)**.

5 Click the **Special** button and choose Paragraph Mark **(Figure 25)**. Word will add one **^P** code to the Replace With box.

6 You're now ready to tell Word to look for all double return codes (the two **^P** codes) and replace the two with a single **^P** code. Click **Replace All** to do just that, and Word will strip all the double returns from your document.

Tip

- A reminder really...the correct way to add space between paragraphs is to use the Space Above and Space Below boxes in the Paragraph dialog box (choose Paragraph on the Format menu).

Finding and Fixing Double Returns

Correcting Double Spaces

As you have already learned, you should never add two spaces (by pressing the Spacebar twice) following periods in sentences. However, if you spent years typing on a typewriter, the old habit may overrule—and you will need to check your Word documents for double spaces. Here are the steps to check for, and correct, the problem:

1 Open the Find dialog box.

2 Click the **Special** button and choose **White Space** from the pop-up menu **(Figure 26)**. Word will add a ^**W** to the Find What box **(Figure 27)**. Word uses the code to search for spaces you make with the Spacebar.

3 Now choose **Special** a second time, click **White Space** and add a second ^**W**. The two codes tells Word to search for instances of two consecutive spaces. *(Continued on next page.)*

```
Paragraph Mark
Tab Character
Annotation Mark
Any Character
Any Digit
Any Letter
Caret Character
Column Break
Em Dash
En Dash
Endnote Mark
Field
Footnote Mark
Graphic
Manual Line Break
Manual Page Break
Nonbreaking Hyphen
Nonbreaking Space
Optional Hyphen
Section Break
White Space
```

*Figure 26 **White Space** on the Special codes menu indicates spaces made with the Spacebar.*

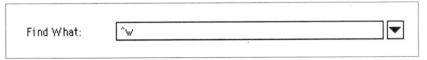

Find What: | ^w |

*Figure 27 Word adds the space code to the Find What text box in the Find dialog box, when you choose **White Space** to search for.*

Figure 28 *Replace dialog box showing double space codes in the Find What text box.*

4 Click the **Replace** button to open the Replace dialog box **(Figure 28)**.

5 Click the **Special** button and choose **White Space** (only once). Word will add one **^W** code to the Replace With box **(Figure 29)**.

6 Now, click **Replace All** to eliminate all the double spaces in your document.

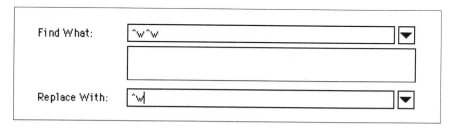

Figure 29 *Find What and Replace With text boxes, showing space codes, are ready to search for and eliminate double spaces.*

Finding and Fixing Double Spaces

Replacing Double Hyphens with Em Dashes

The em dash is used in typography to separate a thought within a sentence. The double hyphen (--) is the typewriter equivalent of an em dash, but the dash adds a professional quality that double hyphens can't match. While you can add em dashes to your document using the Symbol command on the Insert menu, it's faster to simply type your words using double dashes, then replace them with em dashes using the Find and Replace commands. Here's how:

1 Open the Find dialog box.

2 Type two hyphens in the Find What text box **(Figure 30)**.

3 Click the **Replace** button to open the Replace dialog box.

4 Click the **Special** button and choose **Em Dash** from the menu **(Figure 31)**. Word will add a ^+ code to the Replace With box **(Figure 32)**. The ^+ code is Word's code for the em dash.

5 Finally, click the **Replace All** button to replace all the double hyphens in your document with em dashes.

Figure 30 *Two hyphens typed in the Find What text box (in the Find dialog box).*

Paragraph Mark
Tab Character
Caret Character
Clipboard Contents
Column Break
Em Dash
En Dash
Find What Text
Manual Line Break
Manual Page Break
Nonbreaking Hyphen
Nonbreaking Space
Optional Hyphen
Special

Figure 31 *Choose* **Em Dash** *from the Special codes menu.*

Find What: --

Replace With: ^+

Figure 32 *Find What and Replace With text boxes, ready for the Replace dialog box to swap double hyphens for em dashes in your document.*

Bullets and Lists

*S*OMETIMES information becomes clear only when it's changed from a paragraph of text to a list of items. It would be hard to follow a grocery list through the isles of the supermarket if the items were merely a paragraph of text. And, it might be dangerous to describe the steps in working on an electrical appliance in paragraph form—clear, numbered steps are needed to ensure safety. Try following a recipe as paragraphs, rather than numbered steps; or directions to a dinner party as a series of paragraphs. Bullets and numbers can add order, brevity and organization to your documents.

Word makes creating steps and numbered lists easy. The hardest part of bulleting information has always been having to fool with the bullet character. Word simplified the process with the Symbols dialog box that lets you pick out any symbol, bullets included. However, this version of Word goes even further, with commands geared specifically to formatting text as bulleted or numbered lists.

Introduction

Creating a Bulleted List

1   Click the insertion point anywhere in the paragraph you want to transform into bulleted text (or highlight all the paragraphs you want as a bulleted list).

2   If the Formatting toolbar is displayed, click the **Bullets** button **(Figure 1)** to indent the text and add a bullet before the indent.

3   If the Formatting toolbar isn't opened, choose the Bullets and Numbering command on the Format menu **(Figure 2)** to open the Bullets and Numbering dialog box **(Figure 3)**.

4   Click OK to accept the default bullet and add it to your text **(Figure 4)**.

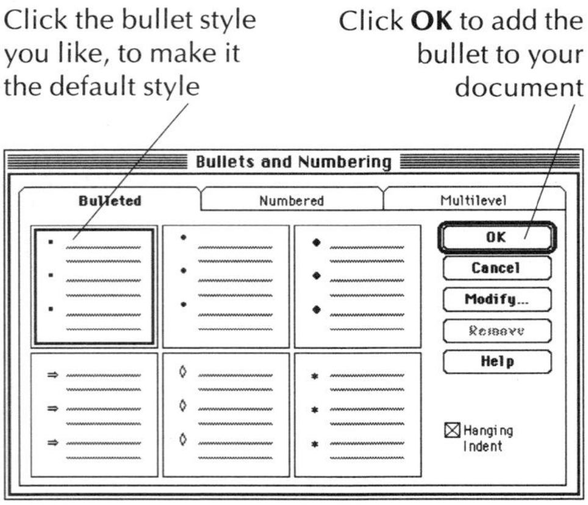

Figure 1 *Bullets button on Formatting toolbar.*

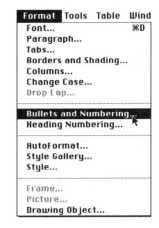

Figure 2 *Bullets and Numbering command on the Format menu.*

Click the bullet style you like, to make it the default style

Click **OK** to add the bullet to your document

Figure 3 *Bulleted tab on the Bullets and Numbering dialog box lets you specify bullets for bulleted lists.*

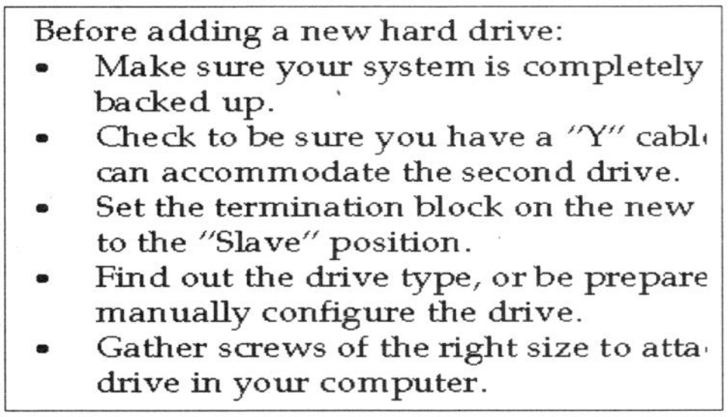

Before adding a new hard drive:
- Make sure your system is completely backed up.
- Check to be sure you have a "Y" cabl‹ can accommodate the second drive.
- Set the termination block on the new to the "Slave" position.
- Find out the drive type, or be prepare manually configure the drive.
- Gather screws of the right size to atta‹ drive in your computer.

Figure 4 *Default bullets added to the text you highlight or the paragraph that contains the text insertion point.*

Creating a Bulleted List

Figure 5 *Numbering button on Formatting toolbar.*

Click a numbering style to make it the default style

Then, click **OK** to add the numbers to your document

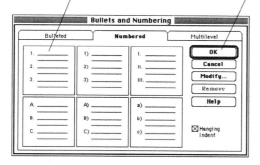

Figure 6 *Numbered tab on the Bullets and Numbering dialog box controls the style of numbers for lists.*

Creating a Numbered List

1 Click the insertion point anywhere in the paragraph you want to transform into numbered text.

2 If the Standard toolbar is displayed, click the **Numbering** button **(Figure 5)** to indent the text and add a number before the indent.

3 If the standard toolbar isn't opened, choose the Bullets and Numbering command on the Format menu to open the Bullets and Numbering dialog box.

4 Click the Numbered tab **(Figure 6)**, and click OK to add the default number style to your text **(Figure 7)**.

Before adding a new hard drive:
1. Make sure your system is completely backed up.
2. Check to be sure you have a "Y" cabl can accommodate the second drive.
3. Set the termination block on the new to the "Slave" position.
4. Find out the drive type, or be prepar manually configure the drive.
5. Gather screws of the right size to atta drive in your computer.

Figure 7 *Default numbering added to text you highlighted or the paragraph that contains the text insertion point.*

Creating a Numbered List

Choosing the Bullet

1 Choose the Bullets and Numbering command on the Format menu to open the Bullets and Numbering dialog box **(Figure 8)**.

2 Click one of the other five examples in the dialog box to make it the default bullet style **(Figure 9)**.

3 Then, add the bullets to your documents.

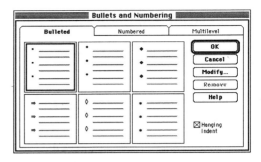

Figure 8 *The bullet style you click in the Bullets and Numbering dialog box becomes the default bullet that is added to your document.*

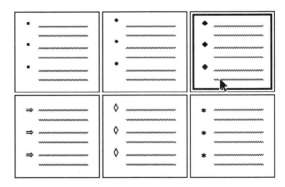

Figure 9 *Bullet style choices are shown in the six boxes: click the one you want.*

Bullet Definition

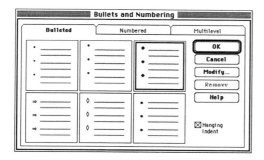

Figure 10 *Click the* **Modify** *button in the Bullets and Numbering dialog box to choose a different bullet.*

Change **Size** or **Color** for the selected bullet

Click **Bullet** to choose a different bullet character

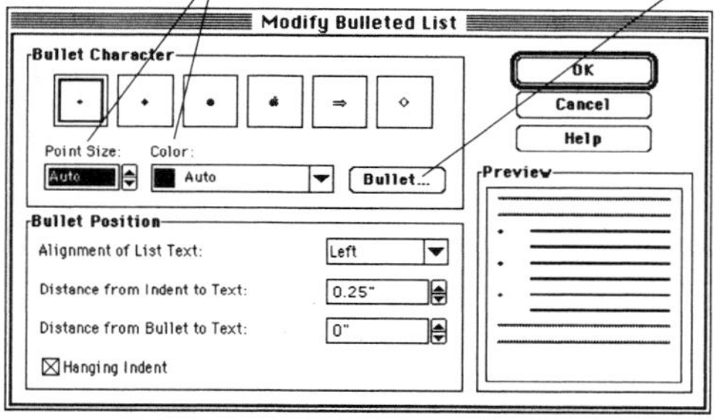

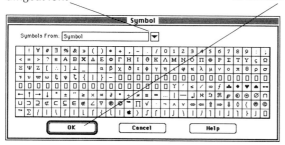

Figure 11 *Modify Bulleted List dialog box lets you alter characteristics of the selected bullet.*

Click **Symbols From** to choose the symbol or dingbat font

Choose the character from the table and click **OK** to add the character as a bullet

Modifying Bullets

The default bullets will suit many of your documents, but you can define virtually any character as a bullet to give your documents a special look. Here's how:

1 Choose the Bullets and Numbering command on the Format menu to open the Bullets and Numbering dialog box **(Figure 10)**.

2 Click **Modify** to open the Modify Bulleted List dialog box **(Figure 11)**.

3 Click **Bullet** to display the Symbol dialog box **(Figure 12)**.

4 Now, open the Symbol From menu and choose the font that contains the bullet symbol you want to use.

5 When Word displays the font characters, choose the bullet you want, and close the dialog box.

6 Now, choose the new bullet to make it the default, and adjust its size by clicking **Point Size**. Click OK to close the Modify Bulleted List dialog and add the bullet to your document.

Tip

■ To make a unique bullet, first choose an interesting dingbat from a font like TrueType Wingdings, or Zapf Dingbats. In the Modify Bulleted List dialog box, select **Dark Gray** or **Light Gray** from the Color menu. You can also experiment with changing the size in the Point Size menu to create an interesting look.

Figure 12 *Symbol dialog box shows a character chart for each font you select.*

Bullet Definition

Modifying Bulletted Lists

<u>**1**</u> Choose the Bullets and Numbering command on the Format menu to open the Bullets and Numbering dialog box **(Figure 13)**.

<u>**2**</u> Click **modify** to open the Modify Bulletted List dialog box **(Figure 14)**.

<u>**3**</u> Choose the alignment of text in the list by clicking the **Alignment of List Text** menu. You can choose left-aligned, centered, or right-aligned text **(Figure 15)**.

<u>**4**</u> Adjust the amount of indent and the distance between the bullet and the list text with the **Distance from Indent to Text** and the **Distance from Bullet to Text** boxes.

<u>**5**</u> The Hanging Indent check box configures the lists in hanging indents, when checked.

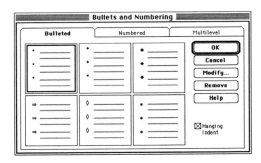

Figure 13 *Choose the **Modify** button on the Bullets and Numbering dialog box to make styling changes to bulleted lists.*

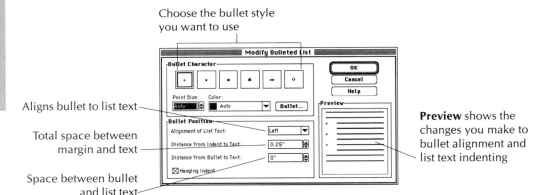

Choose the bullet style you want to use

Aligns bullet to list text

Total space between margin and text

Space between bullet and list text

Preview shows the changes you make to bullet alignment and list text indenting

Figure 14 *Use the Modify Bulleted List to change the bullet alignment, and modify the amount of list text indent.*

Bullets **left-aligned** in the Modify
Bulleted List dialog box

Before adding a new hard drive:
- Make sure your system is completely backed up.
- Check to be sure you have a "Y" cable that can accommodate the second drive.
- Set the termination block on the new drive to the "Slave" position.
- Find out the drive type, or be prepared to manually configure the drive.
- Gather screws of the right size to attach the drive in your computer.

Bullets **center-aligned** in the
Modify Bulleted List dialog box

Before adding a new hard drive:
- Make sure your system is completely backed up.
- Check to be sure you have a "Y" cable that can accommodate the second drive.
- Set the termination block on the new drive to the "Slave" position.
- Find out the drive type, or be prepared to manually configure the drive.
- Gather screws of the right size to attach the drive in your computer.

Bullets **right-aligned** in the
Modify Bulleted List dialog box

Before adding a new hard drive:
- Make sure your system is completely backed up.
- Check to be sure you have a "Y" cable that can accommodate the second drive.
- Set the termination block on the new drive to the "Slave" position.
- Find out the drive type, or be prepared to manually configure the drive.
- Gather screws of the right size to attach the drive in your computer.

Figure 15 *Examples of left, center, and right bullet alignment.*

Modifying Bulleted Lists

Choosing a Number Style

1   Choose the Bullets and Numbering command on the Format menu to open the Bullets and Numbering dialog box **(Figure 16)**.

2   Click the Numbered tab **(Figure 17)**.

3   Choose one of the six styles shown in the dialog box.

4   To change a style, click **Modify** to open the Modify Numbered List dialog box **(Figure 18)**.

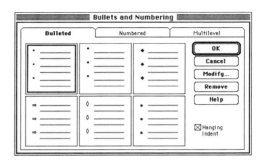

Figure 16 *To select a style of list numbering, click the Numbered tab on the Bullets and Numbering dialog box.*

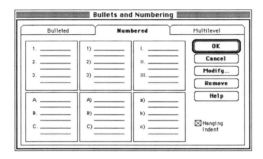

Figure 17 *Numbered tab on the Bullets and Numbering dialog box shows six styles of numbered lists.*

Type the text to be added before or after the number

Choose a number style here

Enter the starting number here

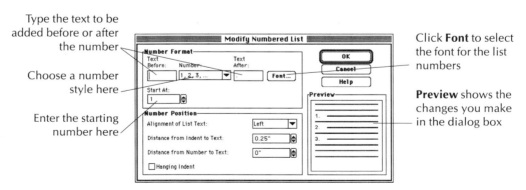

Click **Font** to select the font for the list numbers

Preview shows the changes you make in the dialog box

Figure 18 *Modify Numbered List dialog box changes the current numbering style for numbered lists.*

Numbering Styles

Tables of Contents

*B*ooks, magazines, newsletters, and proposals usually have a table of contents (TOC) somewhere near the beginning that shows readers where to find chapters, major headings, and minor headings. Technical publications will often sport other front matter tables, including tables of figures, and tables of equations. Legal documents will likely contain a table of authorities that cites the case law referred to in the document. All of these front matter tables can be produced with ease in Word.

Word uses styles as the basis for knowing what to include in a table of contents. Simply mark headings in the appropriate styles as you create your document. Then, when you ask Word to create the table of contents, it simply looks for the heading styles and builds the TOC accordingly. Similarly, Word uses the figure captions you add to figures with the Captions command (of the Insert menu) to find the captions in the proper order and create a table of figures.

Choosing a Design

1 Create the document for which you want a table of contents, using Word's styles for headings (to see all the styles Word offers, **Shift+Click** the style menu on the Standard toolbar).

2 Position the insertion point where you want Word to add the table of contents—usually at the very beginning of the document.

3 Choose the Index and Tables command on the Insert menu **(Figure 1)** to open the Index and Tables dialog box **(Figure 2)**. Use this dialog box to specify the style and design of tables of contents, and create the actual table.

Scroll down the Style menu and select the style that suits your document best **(Figure 3)**.

4 Once the style is set, click OK. Word will create the table of contents by copying all the headings in your document and compiling a list in order, showing the associated page number for each heading.

Figure 1 *Index and Tables command on the Insert menu.*

Choose the TOC style from the **Formats** menu

Click **OK** to compile headings into a table of contents

Preview box displays a sample of the style selected in the Formats menu

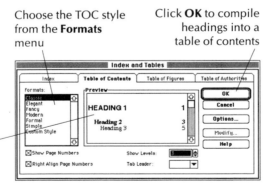

Figure 2 *Index and Tables dialog box lets you choose a present style for the table of contents.*

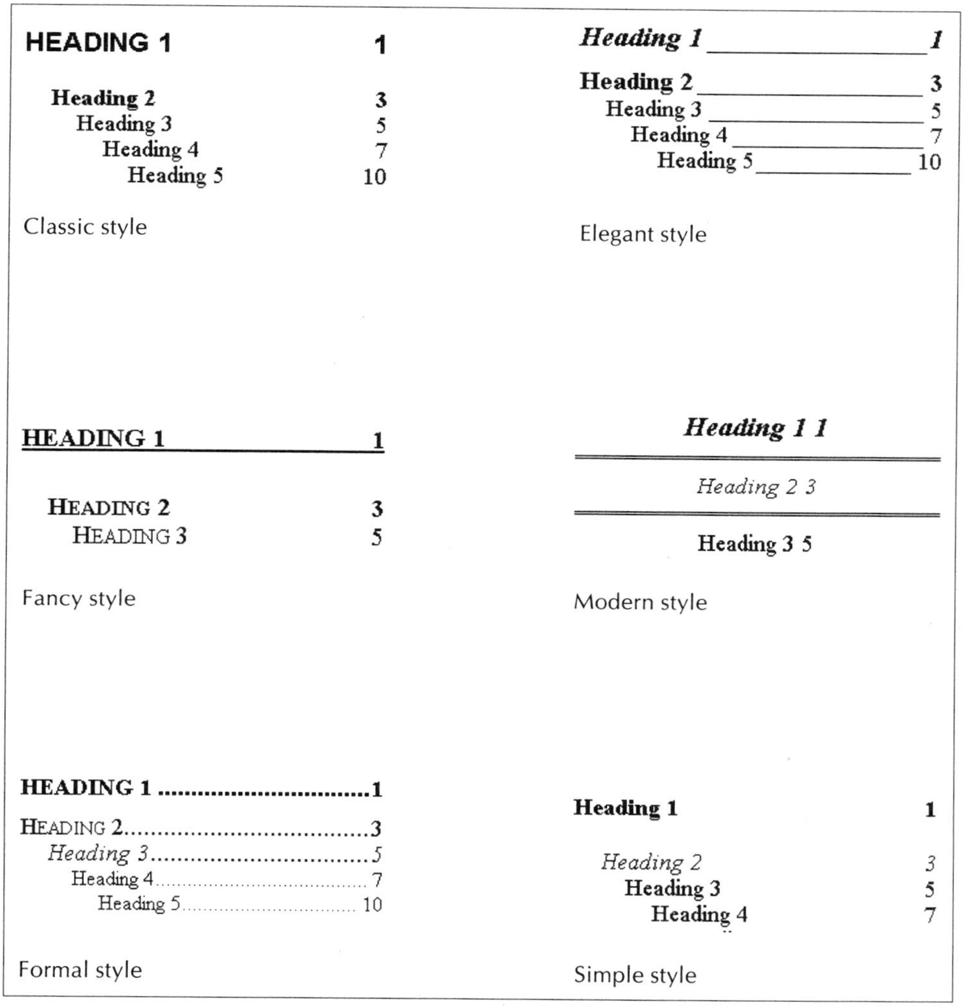

Classic style

Elegant style

Fancy style

Modern style

Formal style

Simple style

Figure 3 *Word's six predefined table of contents styles.*

Adding Design Elements

In addition to the basic design of the table of contents, Word lets you make changes to some of the design elements, like the position of page numbers and the use of a tab leader between headings and page numbers. Here are the steps:

1 Choose the Index and Tables command on the Insert menu to display the Index and Tables dialog box **(Figure 4)**.

2 To turn the display of pages numbers in the table of contents on or off, click the Show Page Numbers check box to add or remove the **X**, respectively.

3 To force page numbers to the right margin, click the Right Align Page Numbers check box to add an **X**. If you leave the check box unchecked, the page numbers will be moved to the ending lines of each table of contents entry **(Figure 5)**.

4 Click the Show Levels menu to specify how many levels of subheadings you want included in the table of contents (you might have four or five levels of headings in your document, but to keep the TOC to a manageable size, only show the first three levels).

5 Click the Tab Leader menu to specify which, if any, tab leader style you want to use. Leaders are characters that fill the space between the heading entry and the page number in the table of contents **(Figure 6)**.

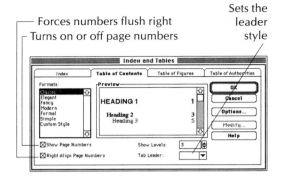

Sets the leader style

— Forces numbers flush right
— Turns on or off page numbers

Figure 4 *Page and leader controls on the Index and Tables dialog box.*

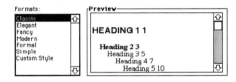

Figure 5 *Page numbers can be positioned flush right, or (as shown here) right-indented to their respective headings.*

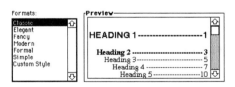

Figure 6 *Leaders (special characters that fill the tab stops between headings and page numbers) are selected on the* **Tab Leader** *menu.*

Design Decisions

Click **Options** to
select style headings
for the TOC

Figure 7 *Word lets you associate style headings with TOC headings by clicking the* **Options** *button.*

These are the
existing Word
heading styles

These will be the
heading levels in
the TOC

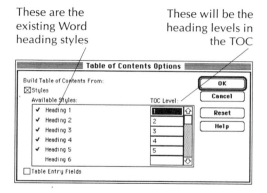

Figure 8 *Associate Word's heading styles with the heading you want in the TOC, using the Table of Contents Options dialog box.*

Selecting Heading Styles for a TOC

You can rearrange the order of headings to suit your needs in creating a table of contents. For example, if you have noted first-order headings with the *Heading 2* style and second-order headings with the *Heading 3* style, Word will let you designate how the headings will be similarly ordered in the table of contents.

1   Choose the Index and Tables command on the Insert menu to open the Index and Tables dialog box **(Figure 7)**.

2   Choose the **Options** button to open the Table of Contents Options dialog box (Figure 8).

3   In the TOC Level column, enter the order of heading style listed in the Available Styles column. If we used the above example, you would delete the number 1 TOC level (which would remove the check mark from the Heading 1 style **(Figure 9)**.

4   Click OK to move back to the Index and Tables dialog box.

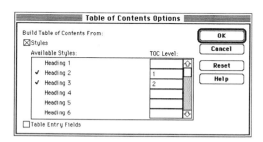

Figure 9 *An example of using Heading styles 2 and 3 as the first- and second-order headings in the TOC.*

Choosing Heading Styles

Customizing a TOC

In addition to the six table of contents formats, you can create your own design using the Custom format option.

1 Choose the Index and Tables command on the Insert menu to open the Index and Tables dialog box **(Figure 10)**.

2 Choose the **Custom** style in the Formats menu.

3 Click the **Modify** button to open the Style dialog box **(Figure 11)**.

4 Choose one of the nine table of contents styles, or click the **Modify** button to alter any of the styles to your liking.

Click **Custom Style** on the Formats menu

Then, click **Modify** to change existing TOC styles

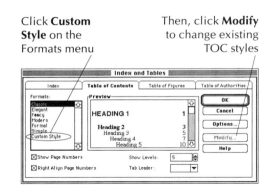

Figure 10 *Define your own table of contents styles using the **Modify** option on the Index and Tables dialog box.*

Click **Apply** to apply the changes you make

Click the TOC style you wish to modify

Click **New** to create a new TOC style

Or, click **Modify** to change the style you've clicked in the Style menu

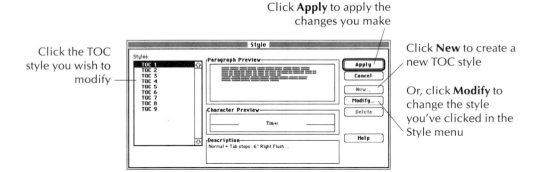

Figure 11 *Use the Style dialog box to change or create new table of contents styles.*

Choose a table of
equations, figures or
tables here

Shows a **Preview** of
the format you
select

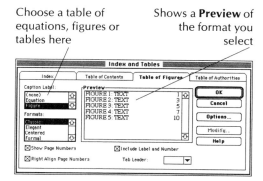

Figure 12 *Use the Table of Figures tab on the Index and Tables dialog box to define front-matter tables of figures, equations and tables.*

Adding Tables of Figures

1 Choose the Index and Tables command on the Insert menu to open the Index and Tables dialog box. Then, choose the Table of Figures tab **(Figure 12)**.

2 Click the **Caption Label** menu to select the type of captions you want to collect into a front matter table: equations, figures or tables.

3 Click the **Format** menu to choose the style of table **(Figure 13)**.

4 Click OK to add the front matter table at the text insertion point.

Figure 13 *Word offers three predefined styles for tables of figures, equations and tables (**Custom Style** defines your own style).*

Tables of Figures

Adding Tables of Authorities

Tables of authorities contain the case law cited in legal briefs. Word lets you create a table of authorities that contains references to 16 categories of authorities, including cases, statutes, rules, treatises, regulations, constitutional provisions and eight custom authorities.

1 Choose the Index and Tables command on the Insert menu to open the Index and Tables dialog box. Then, choose the Table of Authorities tab **(Figure 14)**.

2 Click the **Formats** menu to select the style table you want. Choose from classic, elegant, formal, simple or customize the table to your needs.

3 Click the **Categories** menu to choose the category of citation you wish to compile into a front-matter table.

4 Click **Mark Citation** to mark individual citations for the table of authorities. You will see the Mark Citation dialog box **(Figure 15)**.

Choose the table style in the **Formats** menu

Click **Mark Citation** to mark the text you want cited in the table

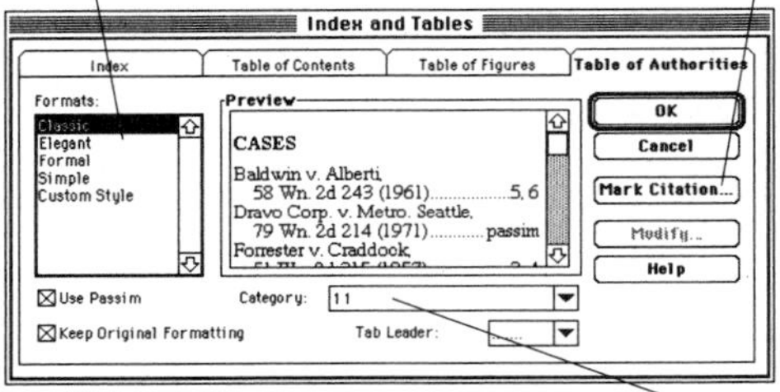

Choose the category of citations for the table

Figure 14 *Table of Authorities tab on the Index and Tables dialog box defines legal citations for front-matter tables.*

Highlighted citation is shown here; edit to create a short or long citation

Choose the type of category here

Marked, edited citations are shown here

Moves to the next marked citation for editing

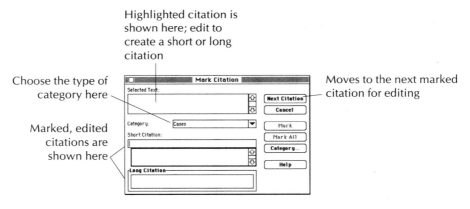

Figure 15 *Mark Citation dialog box marks text entries as legal citations for tables of authorities.*

Indexing

INDEXING is a fundamental part of many types of publications. Lack of an index can give a slipshod air to books, manuals and technical publications, and an impression that the work was thrown together without consideration for your readers. Including an index offers readers genuine help in finding answers to questions. With Word's powerful indexing tools, you'll find indexing easy and intuitive.

Indexing is a complicated subject—it takes time and patience to develop a useful index that really helps readers find what they're looking for. There are four steps to creating an effective index in Word:

1 **Mark entries throughout your document**. Entries should be based on what the readers need to find (not necessarily what you want to tell them). For example, in a publication about handling home emergencies, you think an index entry called "Emergency Medical System (EMS)" would be helpful in explaining how to use the 911 system. Yet readers may find an index entry called "Help" or "911" to be infinitely more useful.

2 **Add secondary-levels of entries**. Secondary, or *subentries* help define a broad index term, like "Emergency Medical System (EMS)" into specific, bite-sized chunks (*Overview, Placing Calls, Street Address Tracking, Recorded Calls*, and so forth). Subentries help readers find the specific information they need.

3 **Add cross references**. A useful cross reference to the EMS index entry might be "See also *911*."

4 **Compile and review the index**. It may take more than one stab at creating entries to get the best index possible. The easiest way is to let Word compile the entries, and review the index carefully—try it out from the reader's standpoint.

It is important to remember who will be reading your document and adjust the index to their level of understanding. In other words, the index shouldn't be more technical than the level of the average person using it.

Introduction

Marking Index Entries

1 Highlight the text you wish to mark as an index entry.

2 Choose the Index and Tables command on the Insert menu **(Figure 1)**, to open the Index and Tables dialog box.

3 Choose the Index tab **(Figure 2)** and click the Mark Entry button to open the Mark Index Entry dialog box **(Figure 3)**.

4 Click Mark to mark the text you highlighted as an index entry. Word will create a hidden index entry code **(Figure 4)** which you can see—as edit—by clicking the Show/Hide button on the Standard toolbar.

Figure 1 *Index and Tables command on the Insert menu.*

Click **Mark Entry** to mark index entries in your document

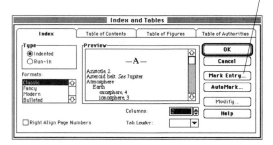

Figure 2 *Index tab on the Index and Tables dialog box handles marking entries and subentries, and formatting the finished index.*

Highlighted text is shown here (change it for the sake of consistency, if you want)

Click **Mark** to add the index marker to your document

Figure 3 *Mark Index Entry dialog box handles the job of marking text entries and subentries.*

Actual index marker

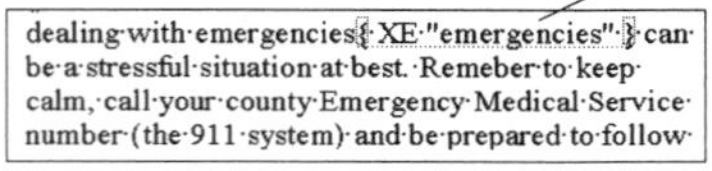

```
dealing·with·emergencies{·XE·"emergencies"·}·can·
be·a·stressful·situation·at·best. ·Remeber·to·keep·
calm, ·call·your·county·Emergency·Medical·Service·
number·(the·911·system)· and·be·prepared·to·follow·
```

Figure 4 *Index marker added to document (whatever is inside the quotation marks).*

Marking Entries

Click **Mark Entry** to add subentries

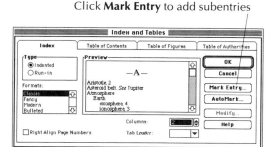

Figure 5 *Index tab on the Index and Tables dialog box.*

Enter the **Main Entry** here

And the **Subentry** here

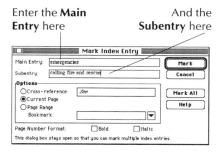

Figure 6 *Mark Index Entry dialog box adds index subentries.*

Creating Subentries

1 Highlight the text you wish to mark as a subentry.

2 Choose the Index and Tables command on the Insert menu to open Index tab on the Index and Tables dialog box **(Figure 5)**. Then choose **Mark Entry** to open the Mark Entry dialog box **(Figure 6)**.

3 The highlighted text will be shown in the Main Entry text box.

4 Type the subordinate entry in the Sub-entry text box. Subentries should offer more specific definitions of the text in the Main Entry text box—the more general the main entry is, the more it needs subentries to help define it. For example: *Formatting Text* (in a Word 6 computer book index) is a pretty general main entry. A better index entry might include these subentries: *In paragraphs*; *In documents*; *Changing Templates*; *In Styles*; *Using AutoFormat*; and so on. You can see that the more subentries you have, the more specific the readers' search for answers becomes.

Creating Subentries

Using AutoMark to Mark Entries

Word can use a simple list of words to create index entries automatically. Word searches for each word in the list and marks the word as an index entry. Using AutoMark, as Word calls it, isn't foolproof, but it can make an easy first step in creating an effective index. Here are the steps:

1 Open a new Word document and create a list of words you want to mark as index entries. Save the list and open the document that needs the index.

2 Open the Index tab on the Index and Tables dialog box **(Figure 7)**.

3 Click **AutoMark** to open the Open Index AutoMark File dialog box **(Figure 8)**.

4 Locate the word list you created earlier and click OK. Word will search your document for each word in the list, and automatically add an index mark for each entry.

Tip

■ You can use Word's spelling program to create the list of words for you. Simply create a new dictionary. As you write the chapters or sections of the document you want to index, add the words (that you want Word to mark as index entries) to the custom dictionary. Then use the dictionary as the word list for Word's AutoMark command.

Click **AutoMark** to tell Word which document contains your index word list

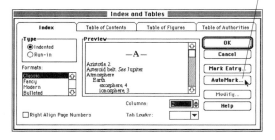

Figure 7 *Activate the AutoMark command with the Index tab on the Index and Tables dialog box.*

Figure 8 *Locate the word list with the Open Index AutoMark File dialog box.*

Click **Mark Entry** to set up cross references

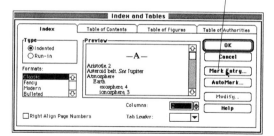

Figure 9 *Create cross-referenced index entry with the Index tab on the Index and Tables dialog box.*

Click **Cross-reference**

Then, enter the reference

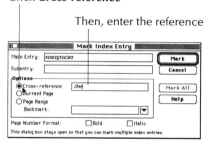

Figure 10 *Enter cross references in the Mark Index Entry dialog box.*

Creating Cross References

Cross references are index entries with a reference to another entry instead of a page number.

1 Highlight the text you wish to add to the index as a cross-referenced entry.

2 Choose the Index and Tables command on the Insert menu to open the Index tab on the Index and Tables dialog box **(Figure 9)**.

3 Choose the Mark Entry button to open the Mark Entry dialog box **(Figure 10)**.

4 Click the Cross Reference radio button and enter the index entry you want to reference in the text box. Use the keyboard shortcuts Cmd+B to bold the entry, or Cmd+I to italicize the entry.

Choosing an Index Design

Word provides six preset index designs for you to choose from. Pick the design that suits you best, or choose a seventh design, called Custom, and modify the index design style yourself.

1 Choose the Index and Tables command on the Insert menu to open the Index tab on the Index and Tables dialog box **(Figure 11)**.

2 Select the design you want from the Formats menu **(Figure 12)**.

Choose the style you want from the **Format** menu

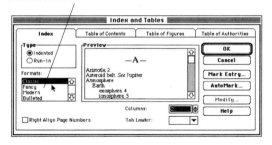

Figure 11 *Index tab on the Index and Tables dialog box lets you choose a predefined index style.*

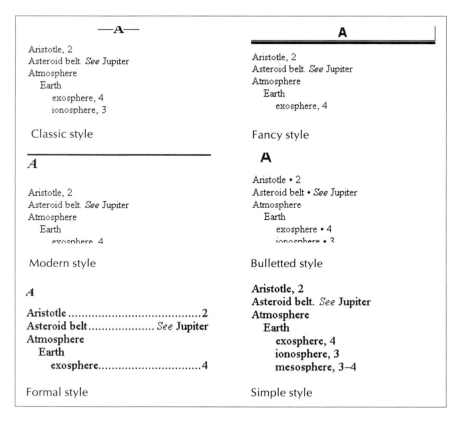

Figure 12 *Word's six predefined index styles.*

Sets leader style for right-aligned numbers

Controls number of index columns per page

Click to push numbers to the right margin

Choose between **Indented** and **Run-in** entries

[Index and Tables dialog box]

Index | Table of Contents | Table of Figures | Table of Authorities

Type
- ⦿ Indented
- ○ Run-in

Formats:
Classic
Fancy
Modern
Bulleted

Preview
—A—
Aristotle, 2
Asteroid belt. *See* Jupiter
Atmosphere
    Earth
        exosphere, 4
        ionosphere, 3

OK
Cancel
Mark Entry...
AutoMark...
Modify...
Help

☐ Right Align Page Numbers

Columns:

Tab Leader:

Figure 13 *Index tab on the Index and Tables dialog box controls design elements for document indexes.*

Figure 14 *Type options control whether index entries are stacked and indented, or run together.*

Adding Design Elements

Once you've selected an index design, Word gives you some choices in how the index pages will look.

1 Choose the Index and Tables command on the Insert menu to open the Index tab on the Index and Tables dialog box **(Figure 13)**.

2 Choose how you want the subentries arranged under a main entry by clicking either the Indent or Run-in radio button **(Figure 14)**.

3 Generally speaking, the page numbers for index entries aren't normally arranged flush right with dot or dash leaders running between the entry and the number (like a table of contents entry). However, if that's what you want, click the Right Align Page Number check box to add an *X*. Then click the style of leader you want in the Tab Leader menu.

4 The default design for Word indexes calls for two columns of entries per page. To have more or less columns, click the Columns menu and choose the number of columns you want.

5 Click OK at this point to actually compile and create the index (see Compiling the Index, below).

Design Decisions

Creating a Custom Index Design

If you're not satisfied with the six index designs, you can create your own design using the Custom format. Here's how:

1 Choose the Index and Tables command on the Insert menu to open the Index tab on the Index and Tables dialog box **(Figure 15)**.

2 Scroll down the list of designs in the Format menu and choose Custom.

3 Notice the Modify button will darken. Click it to open the Style dialog box **(Figure 16)**.

4 For each TOC style in the Style list, click the **Modify** button and change the style to suit your needs.

5 Choose OK to return to the Index tab.

Find **Custom** on the Formats menu

Then, click **Modify** to change index styles

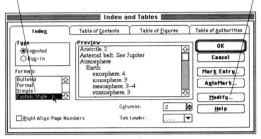

Figure 15 *Create customized index styles with the Index tab on the Index and Tables dialog box.*

Choose the index style you want to modify

Click **New** to create a new index style

Or, click **Modify** to change the style you clicked on the style menu

Figure 16 *Use the Style dialog box to create new index styles or modify existing styles.*

Compiling the Index

Finally, you're ready to create the actual index (you've marked all the main entries and subentries in your document; you've selected a design for the compiled index or you've modified the existing TOC styles to your liking).

When everything is set, click **OK** to compile

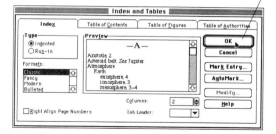

Figure 17 *Index tab on the Index and Tables dialog box generates the index when you click OK.*

1 Move to the very end of your document by pressing Cmd+End.

2 Choose the Index and Tables command on the Insert menu to open the Index tab on the Index and Tables dialog box **(Figure 17)**.

3 Click OK and the index will compile and be positioned at the insertion point as a new section.

Shortcuts to Marking Index Entries

When you're facing several hundred pages of text to index, a shorter route to the Mark Entry dialog box is needed. Luckily Word has a keyboard shortcut already defined **(Cmd+Option+Shift+X)**. If you prefer to click a button on the toolbar, here are the steps to create a Mark Text button:

1 Choose the Customize command on the Tools menu to open the Customize dialog box **(Figure 18)**.

2 Scroll down the Categories menu to find All Commands. The Command menu will appear **(Figure 19)** in place of the Buttons area.

3 Scroll down the menu to locate the command *MarkIndexEntry*. Click and drag the command off the menu and onto the document page. When you release the command it will automatically form a one-button toolbar.

4 Notice that the Custom button dialog box has opened **(Figure 20)**. To add a name to the button (or an icon if you like icons), click the text button or an icon button.

5 To use the Mark Index Entry button, simply highlight the word you want to index and click the button. The Mark Index Entry dialog box will immediately open.

Find **All Commands** in the Categories menu

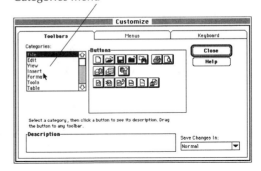

Figure 18 *Use the Customize dialog box to create a command button that opens the Mark Index dialog box.*

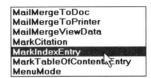

Figure 19 *Find the mark index entry command in the Command menu.*

Click **Text Button** to add a name to the button

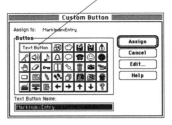

Figure 20 *Custom Button dialog box lets you assign names or icons to custom buttons.*

Customizing Word

V_{ERSION} 6 of Word is certainly the most flexible word processor Microsoft has developed—it will literally bend over backwards to help you and accommodate the way you work. Using Word's customizing tools, you can change the application from a powerful word processor, to a simple writing instrument, or to a dedicated, custom application.

Word can reorder its menus, change menu command names, create customized toolbars, add macros as menu commands or toolbar buttons, and lots more. With Word, you can create a simple word processor for folks just learning about computers, or a moderately-featured program for more experienced users. For example, you could remove all commands from the file menu except the New, Open, Save, and Print commands. And, you could remove all but the File and Edit menus.

Word controls the tailoring of menus, commands, keyboard shortcuts and toolbars with the Customize dialog box. This appendix takes a look at its capabilities and how you can use the dialog box to create your own personal version of Word.

Tip

- A word of caution when it comes to changing menus and commands. You can change yourself into a corner if you're not careful. For example, you could be in the middle of modifying menus and commands and remove the Tools menu. The next time you start Word, you find there's no way to get at the Customize dialog box (which was on the Tools menu). There are two precautions: first, don't make any changes to the Normal template. Instead, create a new document and save it as a different template (choose Save As, and name the document as a unique template). Make your changes in menus and commands to the new template. Second, when you quit Word, you'll be asked if you want to save the changes to the template—if you are experimenting, this is your opportunity to say No, and none of the changes you've made will be in effect when you restart Word.

Renaming Menu Commands

1 Choose the Customize command on the Tools menu **(Figure 1)** to open the Customize dialog box.

2 Click the Menus tab **(Figure 2)**.

3 To change the names of existing menu commands, first click the Categories menu and select the menu you want to edit. For each name listed in the Categories list, you will see a list of commands in the Commands menu. Choose the command name you want to change. Let's change the *File Find* command to the *Look For* command. Locate File Find on the Commands menu. *(Continued on the next page.)*

Figure 1 *Customize command on the Tools menu.*

Then, choose the command you want to change in the **Commands** list

Choose the menu in the **Categories** list

Enter the new name for the command here

Click **Add** to add the command to the menu

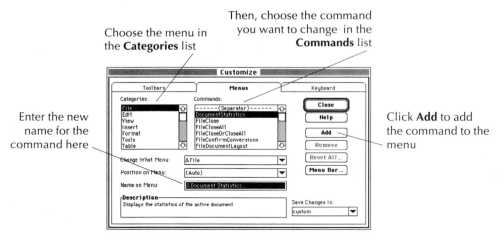

Figure 2 *Menus tab on the Customize dialog box lets you rename commands on menus.*

```
(Auto)
(At Top)
(At Bottom)
------------------------------
&New...
&Open...
Close
-----(Separator)------
Save
Save As...
Save All
------(Separator)------
&Find File...
Summary &Info...
&Templates...
(AOCE Mail Items)
------(Separator)------
&Document Layout...
(List of Print Commands)
Print Pre&view
&Print...
(List of Mail Tools)
(List of Recently Used Files)
Quit
```

Figure 3 *Position on Menu list shows relative position of commands on the File menu.*

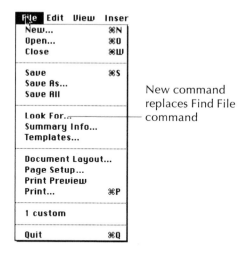

```
File  Edit  View  Inser
New...          ⌘N
Open...         ⌘O
Close           ⌘W

Save            ⌘S
Save As...
Save All

Look For...
Summary Info...
Templates...

Document Layout...
Page Setup...
Print Preview
Print...        ⌘P

1 custom

Quit            ⌘Q
```

New command replaces Find File command

Figure 4 *Find File command changed to* **Look For** *on File menu.*

4 Click the **Position on Menu** list, and choose the relative position for the command **(Figure 3)**.

5 Now, click in the **Name on Menu** text box and change the command name to whatever you want—let's change it to **Look For**. Click **Rename** to save your change and rename the command.

6 Click **Close** to return to your document. Now, open the File menu and see the change you just made **(Figure 4)**.

Tip

■ If you noticed the ampersand (&) in front of some commands, you've already seen how Word designates the keyboard Command Key to activate the command. For example, &Find means if you hold down the Command key and press the letter immediately following the ampersand (in this case, the **F** in Find), Word will engage the command. So to create your own Command key combinations, or to change existing ones, just decide where you want to position the ampersand character.

Renaming Commands

Adding Menu Commands

If you disagree with the organization of commands on menus in Word, you can move commands to different menus, or add or delete menu items entirely. Here are the steps to add a command to a menu:

1 Choose the Customize command on the Tools menu to open the Customize dialog box. Choose the Menus tab **(Figure 5)**.

2 Click the **Change What Menu** box and choose **&Edit** (meaning the Edit menu).

3 In the Categories menu scroll down until you see All Commands, and choose it. In a moment all the commands in Word will be displayed in alphabetic order in the Commands menu.

4 Now, simply scroll down the Commands menu to find the command you want. For our example, let's find the CenterPara command. Click the command and it will be entered in the Name on Menu text box (Word will change the &Edit menu in the Change What Menu box to *&Format* (because the center paragraph command is a formatting command). Just click the box and choose the &Edit menu again.

5 Click **Add** to add the command to the Edit menu **(Figure 6)**.

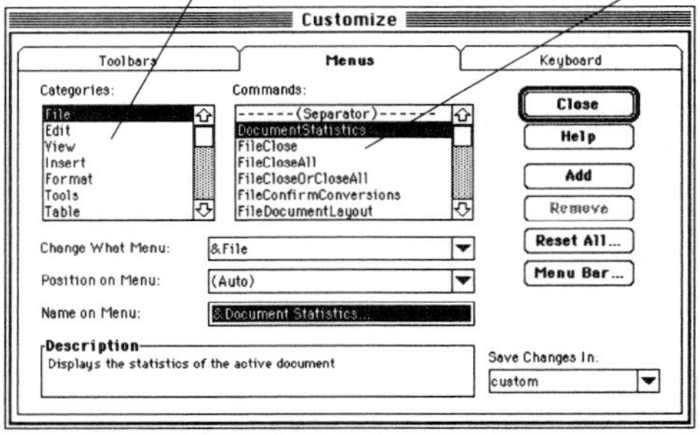

Choose the menu you want to add a command to in the **Categories** list

Select the command you want to add in the **Commands** list

Figure 5 *Menus tab on the Customize dialog box lets you add additional commands to Word menus.*

New command added to menu

Figure 6 *New Center Paragraph command added to Edit menu.*

Click Menu Bar to
customize menu names

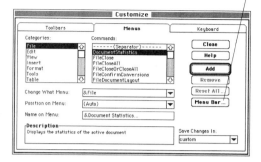

Figure 7 *Menus tab on the Customize dialog box lets you rearrange the order of menus on Word's menu bar.*

Moving Menus around

Word allows you to name menus whatever you want. You can also reorder the position of menus, delete them or add new menus with specialized commands for special purposes. Here's how:

1 Choose the Customize command on the Tools menu to open the Customize dialog box. Click the Menus tab **(Figure 7)**.

2 Click **Menu Bar** to open the Menu bar dialog box **(Figure 8)**. Use this dialog box to control menu names.

3 To reorder menu names along the menu bar, type the menu name you want to be first in the **Name on Menu Bar** text box. Then delete that menu name in the **Menu Name** list.

4 To Add the menu name first, double click the word **(First)** in the Menu Name list. The name will be added to the first position. For each subsequent name, click the name immediately preceding where you want to add a menu name and click the **Add After** button.

Add new Menu
name here

Controls first and
last positions on
menu bar

Shows order of menus

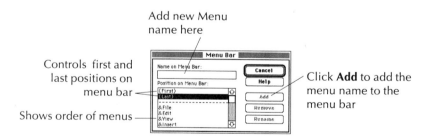

Click **Add** to add the
menu name to the
menu bar

Figure 8 *Menu Bar dialog box controls menu names and their order.*

Rearranging Commands

Simplifying Word's Menus

It is easy to change existing menu names to names applicable to your work procedures. For example, you could change the File menu to *Daily Tasks*, the Insert menu to *Add Forms*, and the Format menu to *Dressing Up*. Here's how:

1 Choose the Customize command on the Tools menu to open the Customize dialog box. Click the Menus tab **(Figure 9)**.

2 Choose **Menu Bar** to open the Menu Bar dialog box **(Figure 10)**.

3 Since we are replacing the File, Insert, and Format menus, let's first delete them. Click each name in the menus list and choose **Remove**. *(Continued on next page.)*

To rename menus, click **Menu Bar**

Figure 9 *Menus tab on the Customize dialog box lets you rename menus on Word's menu bar.*

Enter the new menu name here

Shows relative position of menu names

Click **Remove** to delete the menu you want to change

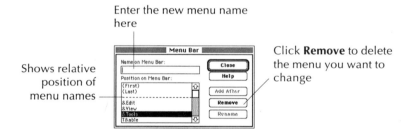

Figure 10 *Menu Bar dialog box lets you change menu names to suit your work.*

Creating Custom Menus

New menu name added
in first position

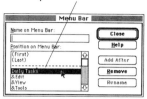

Figure 11 *Menu Bar
dialog box showing
newly-created Daily
Tasks menu.*

Figure 12 *Menu Bar
dialog box with new
menu names added.*

4 Click the insertion point in the **Name
on Menu Bar** text box and type the first
menu name *Daily Tasks*. Then, double
click on **(First)** in the menu list to add
it in the first position on the menu bar
(Figure 11).

5 Add the menu name *Add Forms* in the
Name on Menu Bar text box. Then
click Daily Tasks in the menu list, and
click the **Add After** button to add the
second new menu after the first.

6 Finally, type the last new menu name
Dressing Up in the Name on Menu Bar
text box. Click Add Forms in the list,
and again choose the **Add After** button to add the final menu name after
the Add Forms menu **(Figure 12)**. Before we finish, let's delete the remaining
menus: Edit, View, and Table. Word's
menu bar will now look like **Figure 13**.
(Continued on next page.)

Figure 13 *Word's menu bar showing custom menus.*

Creating Custom Menus

Adding Commands

If you opened your new menus now, you'd find they were blank—you haven't just renamed the menus they replaced, but created *new* menus to hold whatever commands you want.

7 Click Cancel to leave the Menu Bar dialog box. In the Menus tab once again, select the Daily Tasks menu in the Change What Menu list **(Figure 14)**.

8 The Daily Tasks menu will hold some of the same commands the old File menu held. So, click on **File** in the categories list, to display File-oriented commands in the Commands list. Go through the list of command and select just the ones you want on your simplified menu: FileNew, FileOpen, FilePrint, FilePrintPreview, FileClose and FileQuit.

9 For each new command you pick, select its position on the menu using the Position on Menu list, and type a name for the command. Word won't allow you to change the name of critical commands, like FileClose, for example **(Figure 15)**.

10 Finally, click the **Add** button to add the command name to the Daily Tasks menu, which will look like **Figure 16**.

Tip

- If you forget to add the Quit command (the actual command is called FileQuit) to a customized version of Word, don't worry. Even though the command may be missing from all its menus, you can always press **Cmd+Q** to quit Word.

Pick the category of commands

Then the command you want

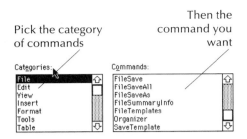

Figure 14 *Use the Categories and Commands lists in the Customize dialog box to locate the commands you want to add to custom menus.*

Figure 15 *Position on Menu list lets you choose the relative position of new commands.*

Figure 16 *Custom menu with its own set of commands, ready for use in Word.*

Creating Custom Menus

Select **Macros** from the
Categories list

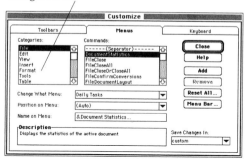

Figure 17 *Use the Menus tab on the Customize dialog box to add macros as commands on menus.*

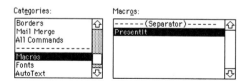

Figure 18 *Macros list shows available macros that can be added to menus.*

Adding Macros as Menu Commands

1 Choose the Customize command on the Tools menu to open the Customize dialog box. Click the Menus tab **(Figure 17)**.

2 Scroll down the Categories list to find and click **Macros**.

3 The Macros list will open **(Figure 18)**. Click the macro you want to add as a command, and choose the menu you want the macro added to in the Change What Menu list.

4 Finally, choose the position for the macro on the menu with the Position on Menu list and click **Add**. The macro will be added to the menu you choose. To run the macro, choose it as you would any other command.

Adding Macros to Menus

Creating Keyboard Shortcuts

You can add your own keyboard shortcuts to just about any Word command, macro, font, AutoText entry, style or symbol. Here's how:

1 Choose the Customize command on the Tools menu to open the Customize dialog box. Click the Keyboard tab **(Figure 19)**.

2 Scroll down the Categories list and choose the category you want a keyboard shortcut for. For this example, let's choose a font. Click Fonts on the list and the Fonts menu will open **(Figure 20)**.

3 Now, select the font you want to assign a keyboard shortcut to. Then click the insertion point in the **Press New Shortcut Key** text box, and press the key combination for the font. Any currently assigned key combinations will be shown in the Current Keys menu, and Word will tell you if the combination you choose is already assigned to something else **(Figure 21)**.

4 Finally, press **Assign** to assign the key combination. Choose **Close** to return to your document.

Choose the category of shortcut

And the command to create the shortcut for

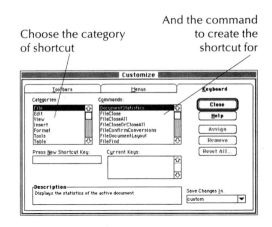

Figure 19 *Keyboard tab on the Customize dialog box lets you define keyboard shortcut combinations for commands, macros and much more.*

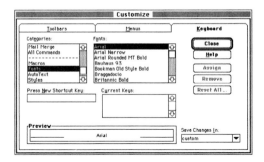

Figure 20 *Shows a font selected for a keyboard shortcut.*

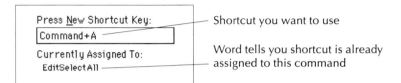

Shortcut you want to use

Word tells you shortcut is already assigned to this command

Figure 21 *Word displays current command assigned to a shortcut you want to use for the font.*

Creating Keyboard Shortcuts

Click the category of commands

Then drag a corresponding button off the dialog box, onto the toolbar

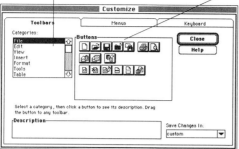

Figure 22 *Toolbars tab on the Customize dialog box lets you add custom buttons to toolbars.*

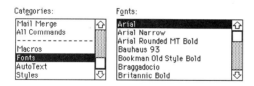

Figure 23 *Choosing Fonts in the categories list makes all installed fonts available to add as toolbar buttons.*

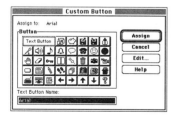

Figure 24 *Dragging a font name off the dialog box automatically opens the Custom button dialog box.*

Customizing Toolbars

Let's say that you use a particular font as your company logotype in correspondence and contracts. Word can add a button to any toolbar to select that font whenever pressed. Here are the steps:

1 Open the toolbar you wish to add a font button to, and drag the toolbar to one side of the document window.

2 Choose the Customize command on the Tools menu to open the Customize dialog box. Click the Toolbar tab **(Figure 22)**.

3 Scroll down the Categories list and choose **Fonts**. The Fonts list will open **(Figure 23)**.

4 Click the font you want to add as a toolbar button, and drag the font name off the dialog box and onto the toolbar behind the dialog box.

5 The Custom Button dialog box will open **(Figure 24)**. Choose one of the icon buttons, or click **Text Button** to add the font name to the newly-created button. You can change the default font name in the Text Button Name text box.

6 Click **Assign** to add the named button to the toolbar **(Figure 25)**.

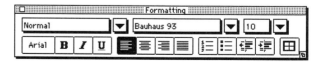

Figure 25 *Finished, customized, Formatting toolbar with Arial font button added.*

Customizing Toolbars

189

Index

Index

Index

Index